HAPPINESS

IS THE

WAY

Also by Dr. Wayne W. Dyer

BOOKS

Being in Balance

*Change Your Thoughts—
Change Your Life*

*Don't Die with Your Music Still in
You* (with Serena J. Dyer)

Everyday Wisdom

Everyday Wisdom for Success

Excuses Begone!

Getting in the Gap

Good-bye, Bumps!
(children's book with Saje Dyer)

I Am (children's book
with Kristina Tracy)

I Can See Clearly Now

Incredible You! (children's book
with Kristina Tracy)

The Invisible Force

It's Not What You've Got!
(children's book with
Kristina Tracy)

Living an Inspired Life

Living the Wisdom of the Tao

My Greatest Teacher
(with Lynn Lauber)

No Excuses! (children's book
with Kristina Tracy)

The Power of Intention

The Power of Intention (gift edition)

A Promise Is a Promise

The Shift

Staying on the Path

*10 Secrets for Success
and Inner Peace*

Unstoppable Me! (children's book
with Kristina Tracy)

Your Ultimate Calling

Wishes Fulfilled

AUDIO/CD PROGRAMS

Advancing Your Spirit
(with Marianne Williamson)

*Applying the 10 Secrets for Success
and Inner Peace*

*The Caroline Myss & Wayne Dyer
Seminar*

*Change Your Thoughts—Change
Your Life* (unabridged audio book)

Change Your Thoughts Meditation

Divine Love

Dr. Wayne W. Dyer Unplugged
(interviews with Lisa Garr)

Everyday Wisdom (audio book)

Excuses Begone! (available as an
audio book and a lecture)

*How to Get What You Really, Really,
Really, Really Want*

I AM Wishes Fulfilled Meditation
(with James Twyman)

I Can See Clearly Now
(unabridged audio book)

*The Importance of Being
Extraordinary* (with Eckhart Tolle)

Inspiration (abridged 4-CD set)

Inspirational Thoughts

Making the Shift (6-CD set)

Making Your Thoughts Work for You
(with Byron Katie)

Meditations for Manifesting

101 Ways to Transform Your Life
(audio book)

The Power of Intention
(abridged 4-CD set)

A Promise Is a Promise
(audio book)

Secrets of Manifesting

The Secrets of the Power of Intention
(6-CD set)

10 Secrets for Success
and Inner Peace

There Is a Spiritual Solution
to Every Problem

The Wayne Dyer Audio Collection/
CD Collection

Wishes Fulfilled
(unabridged audio book)

DVDs

Change Your Thoughts—
Change Your Life

Excuses Begone!

Experiencing the Miraculous

I Can See Clearly Now

The Importance of Being
Extraordinary (with Eckhart Tolle)

Inspiration

Modern Wisdom from the
Ancient World

My Greatest Teacher (a film with
bonus material featuring Wayne)

The Power of Intention

The Shift, the movie (available
as a 1-DVD program and an
expanded 2-DVD set)

10 Secrets for Success
and Inner Peace

There's a Spiritual Solution
to Every Problem

Wishes Fulfilled

MISCELLANEOUS

Daily Inspiration from Dr. Wayne
W. Dyer Calendar (for each
individual year)

The Essential Wayne Dyer Collection
(comprising The Power of Intention,
Inspiration, and Excuses Begone!
in a single volume)

The Shift Box Set (includes
The Shift DVD and The Shift
tradepaper book)

All of the above are available at your local bookstore, or may be ordered
by visiting: Hay House USA: www.hayhouse.com; Hay House Australia:
www.hayhouse.com.au; Hay House UK: www.hayhouse.co.uk; Hay
House India: www.hayhouse.co.in

Published in the United States by: Hay House, Inc.: www.hayhouse.com®
Published in Australia by: Hay House Australia Pty. Ltd.: www.hayhouse.com.au
Published in the United Kingdom by: Hay House UK, Ltd.: www.hayhouse.co.uk
Published in India by: Hay House Publishers India: www.hayhouse.co.in

Cover design: TheBookDesigners.com • *Interior design:* Bryn Starr Best

Material in this book originally appeared in the form of audio tapes of Wayne Dyer's lectures as *How to Be a No-Limit Person, Choosing Your Own Greatness, The Awakened Life, The Secrets of the Universe, Freedom Through Higher Awareness,* and *Transformation,* published by Nightingale-Conant.

Library of Congress Cataloging-in-Publication Data

Names: Dyer, Wayne W., author.
Title: Happiness is the way : how to reframe your thinking and work with what
    you already have to live the life of your dreams / Dr. Wayne W. Dyer.
Description: Carlsbad : Hay House Inc., 2019.
Identifiers: LCCN 2018055195 | ISBN 9781401956073 (hardback)
Subjects: LCSH: Self-actualization (Psychology) | Motivation (Psychology) |
    Happiness. | BISAC: SELF-HELP / Motivational & Inspirational. | SELF-HELP
    / Personal Growth / Happiness. | BODY, MIND & SPIRIT / Inspiration &
    Personal Growth.
Classification: LCC BF637.S4 D8874 2019 | DDC 158--dc23 LC record available at
    https://lccn.loc.gov/2018055195

Hardcover ISBN: 978-1-4019-5607-3
E-book ISBN: 978-1-4019-5609-7

10 9 8 7 6 5 4 3 2 1

1st edition, August 2019

SUSTAINABLE
FORESTRY
INITIATIVE

Certified Chain of Custody
Promoting Sustainable Forestry
www.sfiprogram.org
SFI-01268

SFI label applies to the text stock

Printed in the United States of America

HAPPINESS

IS THE

WAY

How to Reframe Your Thinking and Work with What
You Already Have to Live the Life of Your Dreams

DR. WAYNE W. DYER

HAY HOUSE, INC.

Carlsbad, California • New York City

London • Sydney • New Delhi

CONTENTS

FOREWORD

I spoke to Wayne Dyer almost every day for 25-plus years. He was one of my best friends, and my personal goal is to keep his work alive to benefit others as long as I possibly can.

Wayne is always with me even though he exited this physical plane on August 30, 2015. Writing this foreword with pen and paper, the way he wrote most of his books, I feel his presence through the tingling in my body and the goose bumps on my skin. *Happiness Is the Way* was created from Wayne's Nightingale-Conant audiotape programs, which so many of us loved listening to over the years, and which got me into a whole lot of trouble when I first encountered Wayne.

Hay House was doing a seminar called "Vision of the Future" at the then Paramount Theater in New York City's Madison Square Garden. We sold out the event with about 6,000 people attending. Wayne Dyer was appearing along with Louise Hay and a few other teachers. Wayne was excited because he had dreamed of speaking at Madison Square Garden since his days teaching at St. John's University.

Wayne brought along his wife, Marcie, so they could celebrate the event. Wayne did his usual amazing talk. Afterward, everyone rushed to the book table, hoping to buy copies of his book for him to sign, but the Nightingale-Conant tape sets were the only things we had. He hadn't written a new book in a few years, so his previous books were all mass-market paperbacks, which sold for $6.00 or

$7.00. It didn't make financial sense for Hay House, which wasn't yet his publisher, to purchase and sell them. So we opted to carry only his $50.00 six-tape sets.

The people attending the lecture weren't happy about this, so they went out to the newsstands and bookstores around Madison Square Garden, bought his books, and brought them back for Wayne to sign. They also told Wayne what they had to go through to get his books.

After the seminar, I was walking up the stairs of the hotel where we were staying when I passed Wayne and Marcie walking in the opposite direction on their way to dinner. Right at that moment I overheard him say, "I just want to know who the f**k this Reid Tracy at Hay House is, as they tell me he decided not to bring any of my books to this event. I'm an author, and I need my books available when I speak."

Of course, I didn't stop Wayne to tell him I was Reid. Luckily, we got over that incident and went on to publish many of Wayne's books here at Hay House. After that day in New York, we put on hundreds of events for Wayne all around the world, and we had his books available at every one of them.

Not the usual beginning to a long relationship, but that was classic Wayne: always willing to give others a second chance.

As Wayne and I became friends, we would speak almost every day on the phone or when we were together at one of our Hay House events. If I was on vacation with my family or it was a weekend and the phone would ring, my wife, Kristina, would say, "It's probably Wayne. Go ahead and talk to him."

Later, Kristina and Wayne wrote a series of children's books based on his work, including the *New York Times* bestseller *Incredible You!*

As I read *Happiness Is the Way,* I could hear Wayne saying nearly every word, and I was reminded of what a great storyteller he was and how much I miss talking to him every day.

I hope you enjoy this timeless wisdom from Wayne as much as I did.

Reid Tracy

INTRODUCTION

When you change the way you look at things, the things you look at change.

This was something Wayne Dyer said often, and it inspired us as we worked on this book. The material contained within is taken from speeches and presentations he gave to many varied audiences, over many years. Yet we were struck by how he returned to a few themes over and over again. These themes are woven throughout the pages of this book.

Part I details the impact of your attitudes, choices, and expectations, leading you to a great sense of empowerment when you understand that you can learn to "respond with ability" to all aspects of your life. Part II looks in depth at the concept of success, showing how backward the Western world's idea of it is and how you are likely much more successful than you ever realized, regardless of any challenges you may be facing. Part III explores the importance of a personal mission and includes specific questions to help you chart the way to the life you've dreamed of.

We recommend that you keep a journal with you as you read, so you can jot down ideas to return to later. Each chapter also has an exercise using your journal, to help you absorb the messages of the book. In this way, you'll be left with what Wayne called "an entirely new approach to being creatively alive, healthy, and happy."

Wayne loved talking to people—be it his team here at Hay House, members of the large crowds at his talks, or just individuals he encountered as he walked on the beach near his Maui home. He was always the same: authentic, wise, funny, and loving. He had a way of taking concepts, both profound and mundane, and conveying them in a commonsense way that really hit home for whomever he was talking to. But he also gained so much from other people, saying, "Everyone I meet is a novel." He felt that other people had as much to teach him as he could teach them, and deeply felt that each person contained the seeds for greatness within.

As Wayne will show you, there is no magic potion for getting what you want from life. All you could ever want or need can be found inside you—you simply need to learn to reframe your thinking. No matter what your present circumstances are, you have the power to overcome them. As he said, "Happiness is not a station in life, a place to arrive at. It's a way of traveling. It's a manner of how you traverse the path you're on, walking each step with love." Changing the way you look at things will help you along that path, ultimately bringing you to enlightenment.

We miss Wayne very much but are so happy to have his words to comfort, inspire, and amuse us. We hope this book helps you feel the same way.

— the Hay House editorial staff

PART I

RESPOND
WITH
ABILITY

The trick is in what one emphasizes.
We either make ourselves miserable,
or we make ourselves happy.
The amount of work is the same.

— CARLOS CASTANEDA

CHAPTER 1

ATTITUDE
IS
EVERYTHING

I have spent much of my life studying human behavior. Whether I was pursuing my doctorate, working as a professor and counselor, or writing books, I seemed to return to this subject again and again. In the process, I have discovered reams of material that have been written over the centuries about happiness and humans' pursuit of it. Many people have spent their lives searching for it, thinking that it can be found in something or someone else. That is a fundamental mistake. I have come to learn that happiness is something that we *are,* and it comes from the way we think.

Happiness is an inner concept. That is, you can have it if you *decide* to have it. If you have it inside you, you bring your happiness to everything you do. You bring it to your work. You bring it to your relationships. No matter what, you just have it; you don't have to *try* to get it.

I find that people are often pretty mixed up when it comes to this topic, though. They tend to put the responsibility for how they're feeling or whatever they're experiencing on something outside themselves. They say, "*You* hurt my feelings. *You're* making me feel bad. *You're* embarrassing me. *You* made me unhappy today." Or perhaps they say, "It's all the discord in the world that distresses me. It's whoever is sitting in the White House today that upsets me. The stock market really depresses me." But none of these things are possible on our planet—nothing can actually *make* someone upset, depressed, or unhappy.

If you want to be a truly happy human being, the first thing you must do is really absorb this notion: *Everything that you experience in your life is a result of your perception of whatever is out there in the world.* In other words, you have to take responsibility for all aspects of your life.

To me, the word *responsibility* means "responding with ability." It doesn't mean responding with disability, otherwise the word would be *respondisability*. No, it is *responsibility*: *I have the ability to respond. I can respond with ability.* It means taking responsibility for everything that goes on in your life, which I have spent so many years of *my* life trying to teach.

An Orange and a Candle

Think for a minute about an orange. When you squeeze it as hard as you can, what comes out? Orange juice, of course. But the question is, why does juice come out when an orange is squeezed? The answer is, *because that is what's inside.*

Now, does it matter who does the squeezing? Does it matter how you do it, what instrument you use, or what time of the day you do it? No. When you squeeze an orange, what always comes out is what's inside. Similarly, when you squeeze a person—that is, put pressure on them of any kind—and anger and hatred and stress and depression come out, it isn't because of who is doing the squeezing or when they do it or how they choose to do it. It's because that is what's inside that person.

If you don't have it inside, it can never come out, no matter what your circumstances are. When somebody cuts you off on the freeway and you're mad as hell, it isn't because they cut you off that you're so upset; it's because that is what you carry around inside. And when you stop carrying that around inside, nothing that anybody does can upset you. I love this quote that's been attributed to Eleanor Roosevelt: "No one can make you feel inferior without your consent." In other words, no one can depress you. No one can make you anxious. No one can hurt your feelings. No one can make you anything other than what you allow inside.

Whoever you are, you have a voice in everything that is happening to you. You are creating it. If you're not getting along with somebody at work, if you're having difficulty in your relationships and feeling victimized, if your children don't respect you, look at yourself first and ask, "What is it about me, and what can I change in order to help myself not feel victimized?" Don't default to, "How can I get *them* to change? How can I make *the world* different?" Anything you hate, are annoyed by, or are angry about is really your own hatred, your own annoyance, and your own anger. That's yours—you own it. Nobody else does. It's all on you alone.

When you blame somebody else for being annoying in your life, what you're really saying is, "If only they were more like me, then I wouldn't be so annoyed." As you move along the path of enlightenment, however, something interesting happens: When you encounter the people who behave toward you in ways you used to call annoying, you view it as their problem. You don't own it any longer. You now respond with ability toward those who are behaving in ways you don't like. You learn to tell yourself, "They are who they are, and they're behaving in the only way that they know how to behave right now. So what I will do is this: I will respond to them with what I am. And what I am is love, kindness, and acceptance. If I have that, then I can deal with anyone else's behavior effectively, or I can ignore it. Either way, I don't own it; they do."

It has nothing to do with whether or not you have problems. It has to do with your *attitude* toward problems.

You see, my personal evolution has brought me to the point of understanding that each and every one of us must take total responsibility for our own inner development. And our inner development is something we ignore a lot as we go through life.

Imagine a lit candle: if you were to walk outside with it, the wind would blow out the flame pretty quickly. Likewise, there are all kinds of outside forces you are going to encounter in life that may make you feel as if your inner candle—which symbolizes who you are as a human being—is getting blown out all the time.

But in fact, you can ensure that your inner flame never even flickers. Outside of you, any number of things can and will happen that you're not in control of: the storms of life, taking the form of illness or an accident or any other unforeseen event, may strike at any moment.

Your inner candle flame, though, is uniquely yours. You can always process your world in a way that serves you, rather than in a way that alienates or destroys you. And perhaps the highest place you can get to in life is to understand that your own inner development, symbolized by that candle flame, can stay strong and bright regardless of what's going on out there. Again, I return to the notion of ownership: It is empowering to realize that whatever is going on inside you is entirely up to you. It is all yours.

The No-Limit Person

In the course of thinking and writing so much about the concepts of responsibility and happiness, I have discovered that there are three different kinds of people in the world: The first type seems to go through life full of pain and stress and tension. The second type is not full of pain and stress, but they're also not operating at the highest levels they could. And then there's the third type, who is the kind of person we need more of, I think—what I call the "no-limit person." Like the name would suggest, this is someone who has no limits on their own capacities for living, and who focuses on making their life the best it can possibly be.

Many of the people who preceded me in the fields of self-actualization and psychology have written from the perspective of, *Yes, there are a few chosen people, and they are indeed unique and very special.* I don't think that's true; I think that an awakened life and living without limits is possible for all of us. I have a strong belief that anyone can reach the heights of humanity and operate from these enlightened levels.

When I was practicing as a counselor and therapist back in New York, and people would come in looking for answers to the problems of their lives, the same thing occurred to me as I sat there talking to each one of them. Whoever they were—whether they were attorneys, housewives, or cabdrivers—it didn't make any difference. The answer was so simple. I was often told, "Come on, you make it sound so easy. Why do you do that? It's not easy!"

But it *is* easy. And to this day, I'm still confused whenever someone wants to turn being healthy and happy and together and alive into something that's complicated and difficult.

A woman came up to me one time after I gave a presentation and said, "All right, I heard you talk for an hour and a half, and I got uplifted. But tell the truth—don't you ever get depressed?"

I replied, "No, of course not."

"Oh, that's depressing," she said. "I was really hoping you'd say you did get depressed."

Now, it's not uncommon to see the popular psychologist on talk shows, saying things like, "It's only natural to be depressed. It's only normal to be nervous. It's only human to be unhappy."

As much as this woman wanted me to say something similar, I just don't believe it's only natural, normal, or human to be those things. I think it's only *self-defeating*. We have been taught to believe that we're supposed to be down, stuck, depressed, and given certain negative conditions in life, but that is simply not true.

The host of a television show I was appearing on once told me, "I know you're very positive, but not everyone has what you have. Not everyone has had the breaks that you've had or the intelligence that you have. There are guys who go out there and wait for a bus when it's raining, and the bus doesn't come. And somebody drives through a puddle and sprays water over them, and you expect them to be up and positive at a time like that?"

I said, "Well, I think the difference between being a self-defeating person and a no-limit person is not so much in terms of whether or not you have problems. Every human being on this planet has problems that they have to face every day of their life. We all have to wait for rides when it's raining. We all have to deal with inflation. We all have to deal with getting older, with sicknesses, with our children disappointing us . . . we all have problems.

"But the no-limit person is someone who has a different attitude toward his problems. He recognizes the potential for growth in every situation and doesn't approach the problem as if it should be something different. In other words, he doesn't go out into the rain and say, 'It shouldn't be raining. How come it's raining? It's not supposed to be raining. It's March, and they promised me that it wouldn't rain in March. It's not fair. It didn't rain last March!' This is how self-defeating, ego-driven people talk all the time."

If you ask a no-limit person how much two times two is, they'll say, "Four." But if you ask a self-defeating person the same question, they'll say, "Two times two is four, but I can't stand it. Why does it always have to be four? It's so boring. God, it's four all the time, I get so tired of it being four. Why can't it be five once in a while?"

See the difference? I mean, it isn't that these people are out of touch so much. If you ask a psychotic how much two times two is, they're liable to say, "Thirty-seven," or "Nineteen," or whatever thought pops into their head. Those people aren't self-defeating; they need to be protected!

Let's use another example: a plane delay at the airport. The ego-driven person knows how upset to be because they keep track of these things: *Oh God, this airline! It's five times this month that they've been late.* So they can be five times madder than they would be if they didn't remember how many times. On the other hand, they could read a book, meet new friends, watch planes come in, or go out to the observation deck. Those not in thrall to their ego will do anything other than sit around and complain about the way the world is.

I grew up in Detroit. For seven or eight years, I used to drive from the east side of the city to Wayne State University every day, sometimes two or three times a day. I was a lunatic when it came to traffic jams. The traffic would back up, as it usually did, and instead of using that time creatively, I used it to go crazy: *Here it goes again. I knew this was gonna happen!* Meanwhile, the traffic just kept getting backed up. The traffic doesn't care. Whether you're upset about it or not, it will be backed up until it no longer is. And that's it. That's all you can say about traffic.

Today if I get into a traffic jam, I've got so many alternatives other than to go crazy. Maybe I'll start introducing myself to the people on the freeway. Or I'll start writing, use my phone to get some letters done, or listen to audio programs. You could learn an entire language driving to Wayne State University and back in four years. You could know all of French or Spanish simply by getting a language program for your commute.

Alternatively, you could take the attitude that this shouldn't be happening, and go home and yell at your kids. When they wonder, "What the hell's wrong with Daddy today?" The answer is, "Traffic. Traffic got him." Then you can go and have three martinis.

"Why is he drinking so much?"

"That's the traffic."

"Why are Mommy and Daddy getting divorced?"

"The traffic. It was the traffic that did it, you know."

"How come Daddy's got an ulcer?"

"The traffic did that to Daddy."

Off to the funeral home. . . . "How come Daddy's in there already? He's only 43!"

"The traffic killed your father."

How a scenario like this plays out is entirely up to you. That is the way it is for most everything in your life. Again, you cannot control the storms that threaten you on the outside—but you can always control what goes on inside, and keep your flame burning bright.

How Do You Allow Yourself to Be Treated?

Here's a simple little maxim: *You get treated the way you teach people to treat you.* So if you don't like the way you're being treated by someone in your life, look at how you've taught them to treat you.

Self-defeating people see reality for what it is, but they don't want to accept it. They wish it were different, and they complain about it: "If only you were more like me, then I wouldn't have to be upset at you right now. If only you were something different from what you are, I could be happier in my life. If only oil prices hadn't gone up, if only unemployment weren't the way it is, if only, if only . . ." They look at the world and come to the conclusion that they should blame somebody else. You can tell by the vocabulary they use, by the very words that come out of their mouths. They say things like, "Please don't bother me. I can't—I'm having an anxiety attack."

Now, there is no creature known as *anxiety* in the world, and it sure as hell doesn't attack. There are only people thinking anxiously at any given minute in their lives. And if you can learn how not to think anxiously, regardless of the situation, you can handle anything. Rising prices, taxes, unemployment, losing a job, your children disappointing you, somebody getting sick, someone close to you dying, someone flipping out and not doing things that you want them to do, the stove breaking, all the things that come along with being human—if you can learn how to deal with them, then when a crisis comes along, you'll have prepared yourself to handle it rather than be a victim because of it. If you are always shocked and taken aback, upset over things that happen in the world and wishing that they were different, then you are not responding with ability.

No blame is allowed for anything that goes on in your life. If you get pushed around, if you feel victimized, if you don't know how to deal with certain situations, if you find yourself being beaten down, if you find that your children or your parents are disrespectful toward you, if you can't do well in a particular class, if you think that your boss is on your case, whatever it may be—you are teaching others how to treat you.

I once had a client tell me how miserable she was because she was married to an alcoholic. I asked, "So what's wrong?" She said, "He slurs his words, he repeats himself, he smells bad, and it's so awful to be around him."

I replied, "Let's see if I understand. Let's see who's crazy in this little scenario you described. You said you're married to an alcoholic, and he slurs his words and repeats himself and smells bad and sounds foolish—every alcoholic I've ever known does exactly that. We've got someone who is doing everything that you would expect an alcoholic to do. Then we've got you, and you're married to someone you call an alcoholic, expecting him to be sober. Now who's crazy, the alcoholic who's doing what he's supposed to, or you, who's expecting someone to be something different from what he is?

"He is what he is! Why would you want to keep thoughts in your mind that are making you miserable, which is going to expand the misery in your life by just having those thoughts there? Why not change around those thoughts and tell yourself that if you argue *for* your misery, then the only thing you're going to *get* is your misery. You have to get that you're arguing for it all the time. You're going around talking about how miserable you are—because you have *allowed* it. Change begins with you, not your husband."

Much like I told my client, I suggest that no matter the challenge you're facing—whatever it is you find yourself incapable of doing, whatever obstacle you have encountered, whatever it is in your relationship that isn't working, or whatever is happening in your career—you examine what belief is supporting this behavior. Since the ancestor to every action is a belief or a thought, you can work on changing all of it.

I've done that so many times in my own life. For example, for many years I played tennis every day. I grew up with the belief that I couldn't hit a backhand, and I told myself that fallacy for a very long time. But then I began to change that belief around. It wasn't only that I practiced harder; rather, I began to visualize myself doing all the things that it takes to make a backhand work for me. I began to do that with a drop shot as well, instead of telling myself *I can't hit a drop shot* and then acting out on that. I'm no longer willing to tell myself that *I'll never hit a drop shot* or *I'll never hit a lob* or *I'll never try a spin serve* or whatever.

If you keep telling yourself that you cannot do something, you'll act on that belief. Whether it is improving your tennis game or something bigger, change around your thought. See yourself doing and having the very best in life—you'll find that as you think, so shall you be.

Taking responsibility for how you get treated in life can work with anyone, in any situation. For example, I have found that the way to deal with disrespectful individuals is to let them know that I am not a person who is going to tolerate that kind of conduct. So if a clerk reacts to me rudely, the first thing I do is say to myself, *This is their behavior. They own this.* Then I try to react with some kind of kindness. If that doesn't work, I immediately go to another employee or to a supervisor, or I leave the situation altogether. I will not stand there and be physically, mentally, intellectually, or spiritually abused by anyone, ever, because I know that in allowing this to happen, I have given that person permission to treat me that way.

It's amazing: Most of the time, kindness and love really work to get other people to understand that they can't treat you with disrespect. But if it doesn't, then you have to go to plan B and plan C and even plan D—it all comes from this internal belief in who you are as a human being.

Think of yourself as something so valuable that it should never be abused. Suppose you had a beautiful vase that was worth $1 million: You would never abuse that. You wouldn't play catch with it. You wouldn't throw it on the floor. You would probably put it somewhere safe where it couldn't be damaged.

Well, the same thing is true of yourself. If you think of yourself as very valuable, very important, and very significant as a human being, then you would never, ever allow anyone to abuse you. And most poor treatment—including someone's own smoking, overeating, alcoholism, or whatever—comes from a fundamental belief that *What I'm abusing isn't worth anything.*

Similarly, most people who are lonely only feel this way because they don't like whom they're alone with. If you like the person you're alone with, being alone is never lonely; it's just terrific. Your attitude is that you've got the opportunity now to be with this wonderful person. But if the person you're alone with is sort of contemptible and unacceptable to you, then you'll always be looking for somebody else to fill the void.

Imagine growing up learning not to like yourself, and then taking that self everywhere you go. A lot of people do that, and it's one of the silliest things. You are absolutely whatever you decide to believe. If you're uncoordinated, a lousy cook, poor at mathematics, not very attractive, or what have you, it's because you've allowed that into your life. So if you don't like the result of the choices you've been making up until now, then get off the blame wagon and get on the self-responsibility train. You'll have anything that you want in the way of self-worth because your self-worth is totally and absolutely determined by what you choose to believe about yourself. It all comes down to your attitude.

Each one of us is part of a perfect universe, which works on harmony and cooperation and love. You could never be a mistake, because you are a part of the perfection of the universe. If you believe that about yourself, then when you see other people abusing this perfection, this object of beauty and importance, you'll react the way you naturally would to someone who's abusing something beautiful. You simply would not allow it.

The Secret of Love

Do you know the secret of getting most anything in your life, including success and abundance? It's the secret of love. Yet those who demand love never get it. Have you ever seen people who are looking for love all the time?

They go to singles' bars and are looking at one another, constantly trying to find love, but they never do.

There are several people in my life whom I really love a lot. Do you know how I met them all, other than my family? By doing the things I love to do. I like to play tennis. I used to teach it, and I still get out there and play as much of it as I can. I've met others who share that interest, and we've become good friends. And I met one of my best friends in the world, Maya Labos, running. I absolutely love running and feel great when I do it. She happened to come along, and we became close friends through this shared love.

You meet people by getting out there and being yourself, and love then comes to you; it won't come if you chase it. The same thing is true for money. If getting money is your goal, stop going after it. I speak from experience here: I have gone from total poverty to wealth, and all the money I have ever made, I've made by accident. It never occurred to me that I'd get rich by writing books. Yes, I always worked hard to try to get my writing out there, but I had written six books before the bestseller *Your Erroneous Zones,* and they were all commercial failures. Although those six books had been geared more for classrooms and psychology and group therapy and things like that and weren't failures to me, they just did not make any money.

I also never thought of myself as a failure, since I have always written to please myself. The very first article I ever had published was in a journal called *Educational Technology,* a tiny little publication out of Englewood Cliffs, New Jersey, with a circulation of about seven—this guy and his mother, his two aunts and sisters, that's it. But I didn't care. It felt so good to have my work out there.

I write as well as I can for me. If you buy it and like it, that's a bonus. I never sat down to write any of the books that did become bestsellers while thinking about people buying them. It never occurred to me. It was more like I said to myself, *Wayne, you go out there and do what makes sense to you, which is what you have always done.* In fact, it boggles my mind that somebody else would want to buy something I created. I've been writing for most of my life, and it never occurred to me to do it for any reason other than the sheer joy of doing it. If you really take in what I'm saying, you'll understand what it means to have a sense of purpose in your life.

I'm reminded of the great psychologist Abraham Maslow, who said that the highest-level individuals have peak experiences as their purpose in life. What Maslow meant by a "peak experience" is to be totally, completely, thoroughly involved in a moment; that is, the ability to transcend everything. A highest-level, no-limit person is immensely capable of making any moment a peak experience. There's a sacredness of life for these enlightened people. They are out there doing what seems to make the most sense to them, each and every day of their lives. They speak the language of poets and mystics—the language of acceptance, appreciation, and love.

You can train yourself to have the peak experiences Maslow spoke about anywhere. You can be waiting in a long line, and instead of having a sour attitude and being impatient and upset, you can open your eyes. If you look around and happen to notice a stream of light coming through a window, for instance, this could fill you with joy as you're waiting in that line.

You'll discover that the only difference between a flower and a weed is a judgment. That's all. As far as the universe is concerned, a flower isn't better; some people just happen to prefer them. The only difference between being beautiful and unattractive is a judgment. No one in the world is unattractive. It doesn't exist. "Unattractive" is simply what people decide to believe.

No-limit people intimately know that if any one of us has any suffering going on, then all of us are suffering— it's all of our responsibility. There's a wonderful Chinese proverb: "If you want to think a year ahead, sow a seed. If you want to think 10 years ahead, plant a tree. If you think 100 years ahead or more, educate the people." Once we educate the people, we can raise generations who won't be soldiers, who won't kill, who focus only on love, who see that we are all one.

Even though proximity dictates that we feel more compassion toward the person we know, that's only because we're only thinking locally. When we think globally, we know that an unemployed worker in a foreign country is just as much a human problem as an unemployed friend next door. Any child who is starving, even if they're a continent or an ocean away, affects all of us. A lot of people operate under the assumption that *I only give my love to people who deserve it.* That's a mistake, isn't it?

Everyone deserves love. *Everyone.* Many of us have heard the saying, "Hate the sin, love the sinner." I believe that to be a very important philosophical approach to life. Our attitude must be that the things people do are the things we can help them correct and change. We can teach them not to be destructive, but we must always remember that everybody deserves our love. Until we start thinking that way, we're going to have dichotomies. We're going to always have you versus me, us versus them. As long as there's that us-ness and me-ness and you-ness, there will never be an all of us together. What we need to do is go up in a spaceship together and look down at Earth and recognize that we are all inhabitants of this fragile little planet. Instead of looking for the things that separate us, instead of building more weapons to destroy us, we must begin looking for ways that we can all get along.

As hokey as it sounds, if we don't do this, we won't survive as a species. Or it'll be left to generations billions of years from now who can evolve past the holocaust that we've created, to learn the essential messages of all great religious leaders, philosophers, and spiritual people: that we are love, and we are the essence of what makes this whole thing work. It's all within us. The truth won't be revealed to any of us until we recognize that we're a part of that truth. We're all a part of it, and we're all one.

JOURNAL EXERCISE

Take a moment to think about the concept of attitude written about in this chapter. Then write down in your journal some areas where you would like to take more responsibility in your life. How can you change your attitude and move away from being self-defeating? What do you need to do to become a no-limit individual? How do you think your new views could help our planet at large?

CHAPTER 2

THE
CHOICE
IS
YOURS

I remember being in Germany once, waiting in this Italian restaurant because I had a plane delay. A waiter there, who was directly from Italy, was serving this mouth-watering food. He was also a maniac. Every customer was upsetting him. He kept barking at the other waiters and getting himself all worked up as he ran back and forth to the kitchen.

Finally, I said, "Come over here. Why are you doing this to yourself? Why are you taking this so seriously? All you're doing is serving spaghetti. It's no big deal. If you continue to behave this way every day, I guarantee that you're going to have a heart attack before you're 50 years old."

He said, "Look, what do you expect from me? I'm Italian." As if that explained it. His rationale for his behavior was, *I can't do anything about it; I inherited it, you know. I've got deficient anger genes.* It's like when a kid is failing math and insists, "I can't help it—my father was lousy at math, and so was my grandfather. It's not my fault; I inherited deficient math genes. I can't do anything about it."

Are you shy? Are you nervous? Are you afraid? Are you somebody who can't handle getting up in front of groups because it scares you? Are you someone who gets angry too much? Do you find yourself being manipulated and controlled by other people too often? Are you afraid to stand up for what you believe? Are you a terrible cook? Are you lousy at sports? Well, a lot of psychologists will tell you that it's in your unconscious, and you can't help it.

I was trained a little bit on this point of view, which often puts the responsibility on someone or something else for the things that are wrong with us. That's why you'll find a lot of people growing up in our world with countless excuses for why they haven't achieved success, why they're unhappy, why they can't make something happen, why opportunity has never seemed to come knocking on their door.

A therapist might tell them, "You're a middle child, what did you expect? Certainly, you can't have any identity of your own." Or maybe you're an only child. Or maybe you're the youngest of 12—you had 11 extra parents all your life, somebody always telling you what to do. Or maybe you're the oldest and you had to be a parent for nine others or whatever.

You can use any excuse you want, or you can say, "The devil made me do it," or, "It's God's fault." It seems as if God and Mother are most responsible for all the things that are wrong with us. Mothers really do get a terrible rap in our culture: "It's not my fault, the way I am. It's my mother." I heard it every day for 20 years, so it must be true: "I can't do it. My mother liked my sister better. No wonder I've had such a hard life. She was always the one who got all the attention; I didn't get any. Her picture's in all the photo albums, and there was nothing for me." One night I announced it on network television: "I came here tonight for one reason. I want to tell everybody in America that your mother liked your sister better."

It's all just an attitude. It's what you decide to believe. The fact is, anything that goes on inside you is a choice. Anything in your life that gets in your way, that keeps you from functioning in the way you would like to function, that stops you from reaching your goals—you have chosen it. It's yours. You own it all. I cannot emphasize this point enough: *You are the sum total of the choices that you make in your life.*

Be Confident!

I once had a client tell me how much she wanted to be a dancer. So I said, "Why don't you go out there and dance? Audition for every show that comes along, and take lessons from all the top instructors."

Her response was, "No, I don't have any confidence. As soon as my confidence has increased, then I'm going to be a great dancer."

That's getting it all mixed up. The key to a positive self-image is confidence, and it doesn't just happen. The only way to get the confidence to be a great anything is by first going out and doing it, then doing it again and again. Confidence comes from behavior, from choosing to take risks, from not worrying about failing, from not being so obsessed with whether somebody else is going to laugh at you, from not being afraid to fall down.

Imagine that a self-defeating person and a no-limit person are both climbing a hill, and they fall on a big patch of ice that neither of them expected. The self-defeating person stays there, whining, "There's not supposed to be ice here! Our itinerary promised that there would be no ice. It's not fair! Look, I tore my new clothes, that's not right." The no-limit person, on the other hand, gets up, says, "Watch out for the ice," and keeps right on moving.

Ego-dominated people view failure as something that immobilizes them, whereas awakened people—that is, those who aren't driven by their ego—allow failure to mobilize them. A self-defeating person goes out and tries something they're not successful at, and then gets completely thrown for a loop. They're 15 years old and decide to be principal of their school or president of a national bank. When they're told that the bank doesn't need any 15-year-old presidents, they reply, "See, I told you I couldn't be anything."

The no-limit person says, "Well, if I can't be president of the national bank, I could sweep floors at my local branch in Toledo and see where that takes me." They use their rejections and failures to reframe their thinking, or to go on to try other things.

The essence of achieving self-confidence is doing: *I hear; I forget. I see; I remember. I do and I understand, and not one moment before.* If you don't have self-esteem, get up off your rear end and do anything that will make you feel a little bit better about yourself, and then do it again and do it again. Before long, you'll be a person who has confidence and believes in yourself.

One time, my daughter Tracy was getting ready to introduce me onstage, and she was pretty nervous: "Dad, there's three thousand people in that audience, and you want me to walk out there?"

I told her, "I remember the very first time I had to give a book report in school, what I felt like the night before, knowing the kind of friends I had, who'd be pointing at me like my fly was open and all of the other things that they'd do. I was so frightened and kept saying, 'Oh, please, please . . . maybe the teacher will have a stroke and lose her memory, and she won't remember there's a Wayne Dyer in the class.' Hoping for *anything* so I didn't have to get up there.

"So how have I gotten to the point where I can walk out in front of thousands of people and talk? It didn't just happen. I did it once, I did it again, and I did it again; before long, it became something that was easy and fun and exciting for me. It began with a choice, and you can choose the same thing."

The other part of self-confidence, I find, is not equating your image of yourself with how well you do things in life. *You are not what you do.* If you are what you do, then when you don't, you aren't. You don't exist. If you are your business, if you are how much money you make, if you are your home, if you are your family, if you are your children, then what are you when those things go away? They always do, of course, as life is very transitory. If your self-image is tied up with outside things, then when your job goes, when the house goes, when the children leave, when your spouse dies, whatever it may be, then you die a little bit too.

I've often said that we're not human doings, we're human beings. If we were what we did, then somehow the term *human doing* would have evolved. But no, we're not. We're beings, which means not to judge or evaluate, but to *be.*

If you are what you believe you are, then you'll take risks, allowing yourself to fail at some things and do well at others. You won't confuse your worth with what you do. You'll see what you do in life as choices, but you'll never, ever compromise on this one thing: *You are always a valuable, worthwhile human being.* Not because anybody else says so, not because you're successful, not because you make a lot of money, but because you decide to believe it and for no other reason. If you don't understand that, you won't have a handle on being a no-limit person.

You Can Control Your Thoughts and Feelings

What I'm talking about here can be viewed as common sense, but I also think that it's so logical it almost defies description. I studied logic when I was in college, in philosophy, of course. We studied syllogistic logic, in which you have a major premise and a minor premise, and then you are able to reach a conclusion based upon the agreement of the major and the minor premises.

I've decided that logic is the way to get my point across here. So let's begin with this major premise: *I can control my thoughts.* Next is the minor premise: *My feelings come from my thoughts.* Did you know that? You cannot have an emotion without a thought preceding it. It's impossible. You perceive things in the world, and then you evaluate. This all happens instantaneously. You evaluate, and you have an emotional reaction. Now, people who can't perceive don't have emotions. People in comas just lie there— they don't have any emotional reaction at all.

Let's say that somebody you're in a relationship with breaks up with you, and you feel depressed. But what if you didn't know they had broken up with you: Would you be depressed? Would you be grief-stricken? Would you be feeling bad? No. This emotion will only happen when you find out that they want to leave you. The event won't make you unhappy; it's what you do with it. Thus, your feelings come from your thoughts.

I'm not making the case for being a cold or unemotional person; I'm merely stating two facts. Major premise: *I can control my thoughts.* Minor premise: *My feelings come from my thoughts.* What's the inescapable, logical conclusion? *I can control my feelings.* We can all control our feelings by learning to change only one thing: the way we think. That's it. *I can control my thoughts. My feelings come from my thoughts. Therefore, I can control my feelings.*

Now, what feelings do you have that you don't like? Guilt, worry, fear, self-rejection, approval seeking, living in the past, fear of the unknown . . . these are all emotional reactions to thoughts. And if an emotion is self-defeating, then it is something to rid yourself of as you walk the path of enlightenment.

In the face of circumstances that drive others to madness, awakened people have a kind of calmness and serenity inside them. They're in charge of how they react. They're not calculating, they're not cold, they're not emotionless people—they simply know how not to make negative assessments of the world and what's in it. They practice having healthy reactions to whatever happens, rather than practicing ego-driven behavior.

If the self-defeating person is cut off on the freeway, they let that upset them for quite a while. The no-limit person, on the other hand, tells themselves, "I'm not going to let that person control me today. This is my day. It could be the only day of my life. I won't have it."

If the ego-driven person falls out with a friend, they sit there and stew about it: "This shouldn't have happened. How could they have done this; what could I have done differently? Oh no, I don't understand." The awakened person says, "This is what has happened, and I'm not going to choose to be depressed. I'm not going to pretend I like it, but I'm also not going to allow myself to be depressed by it. I won't. I'll get through this next five minutes. Then I'll get through the next five minutes, and so on. And that's how I'll handle it."

You have to have love for yourself, and really believe in yourself as a human being. You don't need to be insensitive to others, do mean things to other people, or live your life not being generous or concerned or kind. I don't live that way. I don't practice that, and I've never said anybody else ought to. What I have said, time and time again, and will continue to, is this: *We all must understand the power of our choices.*

The Role of Anger

This may sound really strange, but I don't think there's anything wrong with anger. Rather, if it mobilizes you to do something about conditions that need to be corrected in the world, then by all means, use your anger if you need to.

I get angry at starvation. I get angry at children dying all over the world because of malnutrition. I get angry at crime, and at the proliferation of guns in our society, and at the fact that people shoot each other all the time and we don't pay much attention to human life anymore. It doesn't even make the news, all these people shooting each other. But my anger mobilizes me to do something: to speak out about it, to write about it, to try to make a difference by talking to groups of kids in high school, and the like. Mobilizing is great.

It's believed that anger is something that's bad, that thinking angry thoughts isn't healthy. Not true. What is unhealthy is allowing yourself to become *immobilized* by your anger. For example, if you're going through a horrible divorce and are very upset, you can't do your job. You

can't be with your children. You can't get along with your
co-workers. You can't be healthy, and you can't help anybody else be healthy. You can hardly do anything except
get sick, tired, or depressed. That's all you can do.

It's the most irresponsible choice you can make, yet it
has a convenient payoff. You can use that anguish you're
experiencing to keep you from being an effective human
being. It's the perfect cop-out every time someone asks
why you aren't getting anything done: "How do you expect me to get anything done when you know what's going on in my life?"

Guilt is also a terrific irresponsible choice for a human
being to make: *As long as I sit here and feel guilty about what
I did or didn't do, or should or shouldn't have done, then I
don't have to do anything to correct it. So I'll keep choosing guilt
and feel bad. I can only experience guilt now, in this moment,
and the more of it I experience, the less likely I'll be able to do
anything about it. I'll just become this irresponsible, emotional
wreck who not only makes my own life unpleasant and unwork-
able, but makes those around me suffer as well.*

Responsibility is being loving and kind and decent and
good to others—and to yourself in particular—so that you
fill yourself up with positivity and can then give it away
everywhere. Even if there are things going on in your life
that you don't like, you're equipped to respond with ability, to do something, to look for solutions. If you're focused
on your pain and how awful it is, then you'll simply stay
there, stuck with it.

Anger, depression, fear, jealousy—negativity of any
kind—are things that a lot of people spend a lot of time
defending, but they're hardly worth defending at all. It's
very irresponsible to make this choice. Take jealousy, for
example. This emotion is a put-down of the self, a reflec-
tion of self-contempt that a person has. Jealousy means to

take somebody's decision to love someone else or behave toward someone else in a way you wish they hadn't, and to assess that decision as having something to do with you.

Shifting blame in any instance is irresponsible. In relationships, that shows up in sentences like, "If only you were more like me, then I wouldn't have to be upset at you right now. Why don't you work at becoming more like I want you to be?" On the job, it's revealed when managers tell their employees, "I get upset at you when you don't do things the way I think you should do them," instead of helping them understand that there are a lot of ways to do things.

So we've established that using blame is a bad idea, and ruminating on thoughts that immobilize you is a waste of time. Whenever you run into an obstacle in your life and you find that you are upset, depressed, or can't function effectively, then you are in a position to reframe your thinking and change your behavior.

Most people are actually able to handle their anger so it doesn't immobilize them. They can contain it and don't get themselves all worked up. Even so, keeping it bottled up inside can lead to health problems. If you ask me, it's healthier to let out what you are feeling in terms of frustration than it is to keep it in. As long as you don't do anything to hurt someone else, you're better off getting rid of that anger—try taking a pillow and slamming it up against the wall or screaming into it.

No-limit people are able to get to a much higher place, though, in which they are mobilized by anger and use it constructively. What don't you like in the world? What are the things you find really offensive? You don't like hunger? You don't like children dying out there? I personally hate this. The fact that any human being has to die of starvation when we have enough to feed everybody in the world makes me incredibly angry. And when I think about us getting ready to go to war again and killing more and more people, I get very upset.

So what do we do with anger like this? The ego-driven person flails out and finds fault with everybody and yells at them. The awakened person, however, feels the anger but does something about it. They are mobilized by it. They get involved in something like the Hunger Project or Oxfam, write letters to Congress, speak on television, write songs about it, or do whatever they can to raise consciousness about it. They work to elect officials or maybe even run for office themselves to try to change the injustices of the world. They are doers. They take their frustrations and turn them into something good for humanity.

What's Your Motivation?

We all have things about ourselves and our lives that we don't like. But the way that we deal with it just depends on where we are. Most people are what I call "externally motivated." By this, I mean they allow the externals of their life to determine where they're going and what they're doing in their lives.

Imagine if you were to approach a group of down and depressed folks and ask them, "Why are you down and depressed? What's wrong?" Three out of four of these people would respond with something like: "Someone made me angry. They hurt my feelings." "I trusted the wrong person with my money. They made things go bad for me." "I can't seem to get along with my parents. They make me depressed." Whatever it may be, they will use someone or something outside themselves to explain why they are the way they are.

Now, how does a person escape if they are wired with that kind of circuitry? Well, if they blame someone or something outside themselves for getting them down, then they're going to rely on someone or something external to themselves to get up. Oftentimes, the "something" is alcohol: in the United States, approximately 16 million people have an alcohol use disorder. People also use drugs. Or they use sex. They use shopping. They use the pursuit of money. They use anything outside themselves to bring them up when they feel down.

Externally motivated individuals look for approval from other people, use any kind of substance, use explanations and excuses, will blame everybody and everything else for why they are the way they are: "I'm fat because I have to make up for all the starving children in the world. Or maybe it's the food industry's fault. Or it's my parents'. Or God's." It's always something outside themselves.

As an aside, television and social media teach this externality. One study found that the average child in the United States, Canada, and Western Europe spends 1/14 the time in direct communication with their parents and 13/14 of the time in front of a computer or smartphone. That's incredible when you think about it. The Internet is essentially raising our children.

Because children know everything that's happening on their electronic devices, they are taught to be externally motivated. Look at sitcoms: they're a hodgepodge of lessons on how to have disregard for others. Most programs we watch consist of people putting each other down all the time, regardless of whether they're adults or kids. Just watch TV or videos online, and you'll see smart-alecky remarks and very little regard for human dignity, broken up by innumerable commercials for products that encourage external motivation.

✺

While there are a great number of human beings who are externally motivated, some have a combination of external *and* internal motivations. These people do have some inner directedness. When things are not going well, they know in their hearts that they're responsible for the situation, but they don't seem to have a handle on what to do about it. Again, this leads to a sense of being immobilized.

Take war, for example. Wars are caused by nonconstructive anger, and people responding with nonconstructive anger, and they often go on and on in this way for years. How many people are against terrorism? I mean, who *isn't* against it? We are all against terrorism—but ironically, that is one of the reasons we continue to have terrorists and war in the world. Because so many people are against it. Imagine if everybody who was against terrorism would phrase it in terms of "I am for peace," and redirect that same energy. If millions of people worked *for* peace instead of *against* terrorism, we would have a peaceful world.

If you look at the statistics, for every $1 we spend on peace, we spend $2,000 on war. That is why we have guns and ammunition and bombs and nuclear weapons and all the things that could destroy us. We are always focused on what we are *against* instead of what we are *for*, and it ultimately immobilizes us. Likewise, you hear people talking about a war on drugs. As soon as you have a war, you have to choose sides. You need a winner and a loser, and you have to have armaments. The drugs will continue to go on as long as there is a war. I think we could phrase it in a positive way, to focus on having a drug-free culture.

Shifting our thinking in such a way means that we're responding to internal motivation, rather than external. Try this in your own life, looking at the areas that you'd like to improve. Maybe you would like to be less dogmatic in your relationship with your partner. Instead of putting it into a negative, look to frame it as an affirmation, using present-focused, "I am" phrases: *I am becoming a more pleasant person.* Instead of berating yourself for being tardy all the time, try: *I am working on arriving on time.* Instead of bemoaning the fact that you don't spend enough time with your kids, tell yourself: *I am devoting lots of time to my children.* Instead of procrastinating, affirm*: I am spending more time working on this particular project that I am so interested in.*

In other words, you shift from being immobilized by your negativity, thinking of yourself as flawed, and instead begin to state things in a positive way. Remember, our flawless universe works on harmony, and it does not make any mistakes. It is a perfect system, and each one of us is a part of this perfection. See yourself in that way, and then see yourself as making new choices for your evolution, rather than repairing faults and deficiencies. You will see yourself growing and growing, and the things that used to immobilize you—that depressed you and got you upset, that you used to call flaws—are no longer seen as such. They are now seen as choices that you made along the way.

Choosing to Grow

The concept of choice making is so important to me that my friends think it's almost like an obsession. I really believe that we are much more capable in this area than we think. In my heart, in my soul, in everything that I am, I believe that we all have the power to choose and control and direct our own destiny. However it came to us, be it from God or evolution, we have free will. It would be the ultimate cruelty to believe that we indeed have free will but it's only an illusion. That in fact everything is all programmed for us, and we're just living out someone else's script. No. I have free will because I am part of all of humanity. I am at once unique and special, while also a part of humanity at the same time.

Now, what can we do to improve our human condition? First and foremost, there are no problems that are defined by nationalism. They're defined by human qualities, not how we fit people in and slot them and compartmentalize them. Growth-minded people understand this. They have the ability to look holistically, saying things like, "Let's make this planet a better place for all of us so that we eliminate the possibilities for war and killing. Let's start with not even thinking about killing anything that's alive, unless it's absolutely necessary as part of a food chain. Let's have sacredness for all living things."

These individuals seem to be motivated by the highest possible needs: The need for truth. The need for love. The need for identification and feeling of belonging as a human being. The need for dignity. These things run their lives. Their lives are not consumed by *How am I doing today? What am I getting for myself? How is all of this fitting in for me?*

You see, we think that the need for food is more important than the need for truth. Have you ever spent any time around people who do nothing but lie? You take away truth and beauty and a sense of dignity from people, and it's going to kill them as dead as if you take their food away—it's just going to take a little longer. Enlightened, internally motivated men and women understand this. They are able to transcend their own egos and are spiritual in nature. They are more identified with what is really right about humanity. When you're around people like this, there is such a sense of inspiration, of wanting to be closer to them and not being able to get enough. It becomes infectious.

They are innovators, discoverers of the new, and they don't go along with the way things always used to be. Think about cooking. If we all did things the way we always did, then there would be one cookbook in the world, and it would have one recipe in it: *Take one whole antelope. Build one great big bonfire, and throw it on top. That's it.*

Innovators, on the other hand, say, "Well, wait a minute. Maybe we ought to skin the antelope first. Or let's sauté it a little. Or let's check out its flanks or whatever." These people will swim against the current: "No, I don't think I'll do it that way. Instead, I'm going to try it this way. I'll add a little of this. I'll add a little of that. I'll add my own twist to it." They have the ability and the willingness to try something unique and apply that uniqueness to anything they do, and that's what creativity is. They have an appreciation for the mysterious in life. They want to try new things. They want to go after things they've never done before instead of spending their lives doing what they've always done.

No-limit people have what is called unconflicted love. You see, the greatest cause of stress in our world is being in an unresolved relationship: Not a divorce. Not a change of career. Not losing a job. Not losing someone close to you. It is living in a relationship that you know is unresolved. This is when you find yourself thinking things like, *I don't know if I'm going to get there, if this is where I should or shouldn't be. I don't know. I'm thinking about it. I'm hoping that he'll change. I'm waiting. I've been waiting 28 years. He still hasn't changed. Maybe things will get better one day . . .* and on and on.

Living like that, whether it's been 28 years or 28 hours, just saps the energy right out of you. Moving to unconflicted love means that you think like this: *I look out in the world and see people I love. Unconditionally, in an unconflicted way, I can say "I love you" to anyone I come across. No one has to meet my expectations, and I don't want to be told to meet theirs.* If you can pass that test, you're in unconflicted love. If you're not, resolve it. Whether it's getting back together with someone, making your current relationship work on a daily basis, or deciding to finally get the hell out of it, you will be in a better position once you make a decision and can enjoy unconflicted love.

Awakened people are motivated by growth rather than a sense of lack or deficiency. Those kinds of people are the ones who are going to make this planet operate at a higher level—and we can all strive for the same thing. You may currently feel that you're motivated by your deficiencies, thinking, *I want to improve myself, so I'll do this.* But keep in mind that you don't have to be sick to get better. You don't have to look at yourself as in bad shape in order to grow.

Everything in the universe is exactly as it should be. So stop judging it, including the part that is yourself, and go to work. Resolve the things that you don't like and accept those you can do nothing about. Run your life on this concept: *Each day is great. Where I am is just fine, and so is where I'm going.* That's called growth motivation, and it's a choice you can make right now.

JOURNAL EXERCISE

Think about reframing the negative statements that frequently go through your mind by turning them into positive affirmations. For example, instead of *I'm so broke,* try *I am enjoying a life of prosperity.* Or instead of *I hate my job,* try *I am very happy in my fulfilling career.* Write a few of these positive statements down in your journal, and then post them where you can see them throughout the day—such as on your bathroom mirror, your computer monitor, or the dashboard of your car. In this way, you will learn to train your brain to focus only on the good, and then attract it into your life.

CHAPTER 3

WHAT DO YOU EXPECT?

Before I go out to speak in front of an audience, I tend to hear variations on this theme: "You're going to talk for four hours? Boy, are you going to be tired when you finish. You're going to be exhausted!" I typically reply, "What for? No, I am not going to be exhausted. I don't think tired—that has nothing to do with any way my mind is organized."

There are so many people who get into bed at two o'clock in the morning and tell themselves, *Oh my gosh, it's already two. I've got to get up at six. That's only four hours from now. If I were to fall asleep right this second, and I'm not even close, I'll hardly get any rest. . . . Oh, am I going to be tired tomorrow.* They lie there and toss and turn and get themselves all worked up, and sure enough, 45 minutes go by. *Now it's a quarter to three. Quarter to four. Quarter to five. Quarter to six.* Now they upgrade: *I'm going to be a zombie today!*

It's how expectations work. When the alarm goes off, whatever you've had in mind will decide what your day is going to be like. Put your body on *droop;* put your eyes on *bag.* As soon as you get into work, you say, "Don't talk to me; I got no sleep last night. I'm sure I'll be a zombie today. This is going to be a bad day." You see?

People organize their expectations to set themselves up for a negative outcome, instead of saying to themselves, *Okay, I'm never going to be tired again in my life. I'm simply not going to have tired thoughts. If my bones ache a bit, if I get a little drowsy or whatever, I will either take a quick nap or just shake it off and go for a walk. I won't tell anybody else how tired I am. Mostly because nobody wants to hear it anyway.* If you think they do, try asking around: "Excuse me, do you care how tired I am?" You'll find that no one wants to hear about it.

So get that expectation of being tired out of your mind completely, and don't think that way unless you have to go maybe three or four days without sleep. Then you can tell yourself, *All right, I'm entitled to be tired.*

Your expectations determine so much about your life. For example, they determine how physically healthy you are, whether you have colds and backaches and headaches and cramps and things like that. See if this sounds famil-iar: *Oh boy, here comes that cold that's been going around. It's only in my nose now, but it'll be down in my chest by Monday. By Wednesday, I'll have a fever; I'll have to take next Thursday and Friday off. I know it's only Saturday now, but it always happens that way.* You set yourself up to be sick.

Another option would be to tell yourself: *This is a mis-take. I'm not interested in this. I don't want it. This a cue to me that I need to take a few extra tablets of vitamin C and get a little more rest, but I'm not going to tell anybody else about it. I'll see if I can go through this whole thing without letting any-body else know I've got it. I'm also going to keep myself active. I'm not going to focus on this or let it get in the way of anything I'm doing.*

I had a friend who was learning to skydive. He had a really bad cold, but he couldn't postpone his first jump. I drove him to the site, and on the way there, he couldn't stop talking about how awful he felt, and he couldn't believe he'd have to jump in his state. Nevertheless, I dropped him off, and he went to join his class. For two hours he was occupied with all that he had to do to prepare to jump, and there were too many things to do to be sick. After all, if you're falling through the air on the way to the ground, you really don't want to be bothered with a cold.

My friend jumped once, but he wasn't satisfied with it. So he went back up and did it again. As we got in the car after I picked him up, I asked how it had gone. All of a sudden, he didn't have a cold. He said, "I'll be darned. Ain't that something?" It wasn't as if he hadn't been thinking about it but still had somebody wiping his nose for him. The cold was no longer there at all—he didn't have it. It seems to me that there's a lesson in that.

You Are Not Your Form

I was on an airplane and had with me a baby carriage that I was bringing to my brother and sister-in-law. When the flight attendant saw it, she asked me, "Is that for your granddaughter?"

I thought to myself, *How could she possibly think that someone as young as I am could be a grandfather? How could a 14-year-old be a grandfather?* That's my perception of myself: I see myself as a little boy. I sure act like one. I run every day, and I play tennis better than I ever have before. I can do almost anything that I want to. I know it isn't the age of our bodies that counts because none of us are our bodies. We are our conscious awareness. What we are is intangible; after all, we've occupied many different bodies already while on this planet.

I was in an eight-pound body, and I was in a body that was only two and a half feet tall. I was in a body that didn't have any hair on it, and then it had a whole bunch of hair on it, and then it all fell out again later on. I've been in lots of different bodies. But nothing about me—not one physical cell that was in any of those bodies—is in the body that I carry now. Every cell has been changed . . . yet I can remember everything about what I did when I was 10 years old. I am not a body with a soul; I'm a soul with a body.

Remember, attitude is everything! Understand that your aging is not the condition of your body, because you are not your body. You are thought. Having your physical form get older is one thing, but *you* don't have to get older. It's just a way of looking at your life. Yes, your body will slow down, and it won't be able to do the things that it could do at one time—but again, most of that is controlled by your thinking. If you focus solely on your body, then you will notice everything about it that is changing and assess it in a way that says, *I am deteriorating*. But if what you are is not your body but your thoughts, then you can never deteriorate. After all, you can't kill thoughts. You can't kill feelings. You can only kill form. And if you know that you are not that form, then you know that your conscious awareness can never die.

I see such a miracle in this whole business called life, and that doesn't have to change because my form is growing older. The way I look at it, I have a child inside me. I choose to think that of myself regardless of what anybody else thinks, even if a flight attendant thinks that a baby carriage could be for my granddaughter. If that's what she thinks, that's just what she thinks. *I* don't think that way, and that's what matters. I don't see any effects of my form getting older. Every once in a while I notice a new little wrinkle or other changes that have taken place in my body, but that is not *what* I am.

I don't assess my value and worth as a human being based on my body. I do treat it in very healthful ways: I eat a third of what I used to eat in total bulk in a given day. The only sugar I consume comes naturally from fruits. I don't add salt to my food. I walk almost everywhere I go instead of getting in a car and being driven someplace. I run several miles every single day. Yet I didn't decide to do any of this out of a fear that my body was getting older, so I needed to take better care of it.

Rather, this is all the result of my being in a higher state of pure thought, of self-acceptance. I see myself as an important, significant human being—but I also see other people and the whole world in this more purified, more loving kind of way. In other words, my body is able to stay in remarkable shape because of the way I think.

I bet that if you also keep a strong grip on the way that you think and process your world, you'll see your body getting healthier and more capable than you ever thought it would be as well. Even the total wearing out of your body is an attitude. I really do think this.

It seems as if people begin preparing themselves for death from the time they learn there is such a thing. If we didn't prepare ourselves for death and getting sick and slowing down, then our bodies wouldn't have to wear out. There's something in the aging process that has to do with our consciousness of it. Once we have learned how to transcend the kinds of thoughts that prepare us for getting older and feebler, I believe we will have conquered the aging process.

We all have within us the capacity to do great things and overcome any obstacle. This makes me think of Norman Cousins, who wrote the book *Anatomy of an Illness as Perceived by the Patient*. Cousins had been diagnosed with ankylosing spondylitis, an inflammatory disease that can cause some of the vertebrae in the spine to fuse. When told he had something like a 1-in-500 chance of even surviving it, let alone ever walking again, Cousins decided he absolutely was not going to give in. He vowed to keep himself internally motivated, which he accomplished by using laughter. I don't think we've researched the importance of laughter enough, how good it feels to laugh and how therapeutic it is to be able to laugh at ourselves and others and not take life so seriously. Not having a stony kind of grimness about ourselves is invaluable.

Cousins arranged to have all the things that he ever thought were funny in his life sent to his hospital bedroom, such as films featuring the Marx Brothers and Abbott and Costello. He played these movies over and over again, and he experienced this raucous kind of gut laughter day after day. This, combined with his general attitude and belief, helped him heal. Most doctors, surgeons in particular, know that the patient who has a will to live and survive has got a greater chance of surviving and thriving than the patient who feels down and depressed, who's already given up.

We can't define what that will is. We can't put a statistical mark on it, but we know it's there. We've all heard stories about mothers doing heroic things to rescue their children, be it lifting up cars by themselves to free a child who's trapped or pulling their children out of a burning building. Within each one of us is that kind of capacity, and we haven't even begun to tap into it.

Here's what I mean by this: you can make a commitment to something as basic and simple as whether or not you're going to be sick anymore, or how much you're going to allow some illness to have control over you. To what extent are you going to permit it to immobilize you, to keep you down? Television tells you when to get a cold because they want to sell you cough medicine or nose spray or whatever it is they're advertising. But you can make that decision for yourself; after all, you are not your form.

How Healthy Can You Be?

One of my arguments with the way medicine is practiced in the world today can be seen if we imagine a line with three points: A, B, and C. Point A represents illness, an absence of health. Point B represents "normal"—that is, nothing's wrong with us. Point C represents complete possibilities, total potential for health. This is as healthy as we can get.

Almost all medicine in the United States is practiced between points A and B. You don't see a doctor unless you've got something wrong with you, and then you go and tell them about your symptoms. "I've got sniffles, I've got a fever, my arm hurts," whatever it may be. This is the way Western medicine is practiced—getting you from your affliction to where you don't have any more symptoms.

There's another way to do it, which is actually how most medicine should be practiced, in my view. Certainly, if you have a gallbladder that needs to be taken out, you should have it taken out. But for the most part, focusing on the area between point B (which is feeling normal) and point C (which is your maximum potential for health) would be a fantastic way to practice medicine. Preventive, holistic, humanistic, behavioral medicine is starting to gather momentum across the United States, and that's wonderful. But imagine that you were able to use the field of medicine in terms of *getting healthier* instead of *getting rid of sickness.* How healthy can you possibly be?

What do you expect is possible for you as a human being? Do you ever think about that? How many vitamins can you be getting? How can you get yourself to where you could run 50 miles without feeling tired? Can you exercise all day and love it? Can you walk up 20 flights of stairs and not even be breathing hard? Can you go for a long, strenuous hike in the woods and feel great?

A medicine of being—a holistic, humanistic approach to treating people—is such a brilliant idea. When you work from an awakened, transformed point of view, you do this all the time. You're always thinking of how healthy you can be. You don't see a symptom as a reason to go off to the doctor or pop some pills; you don't want to have somebody else tell you what's wrong with you by pouring more and more drugs into you. Now, I am not putting down modern medicine. I respect physicians immensely; they are without a doubt our best-trained professionals. But I think there's great benefit in not just treating people physically, but also training them from a young age to grow up thinking and acting as healthy as they can be.

Imagine raising your kids to think this way. . . . You wouldn't complain about them eating junk food because it wouldn't be there. You wouldn't need to have that in your house. You'd model running, walking, bicycling, swimming, and doing other physically active things together.

You'd feel incredibly healthy. You wouldn't think sickness, allergies, or the like. Imagine that.

One of the things that we tend to do in families is reward children for being sick. We pay more attention to them, we cuddle them, we let them stay home from school, we put wraps around them, we bring a television in to them, we bring them the soda pop they may not otherwise get. We go in and talk to them all the time, we feel their forehead, we massage them. We essentially punish them for being well, which is the exact opposite of how you would want to reinforce given behaviors.

What if you sent your doctor a check every month as long as you were well, but he'd get no payment if you were sick because his job was to promote wellness and not sickness? I think that same logic can apply in the raising of our kids. That's why when any of my children tell me they don't feel well or are getting a cold or whatever, my initial reply is always, "Oh, you're not going to get that cold. You're too strong for that. You are so fantastic. You are such a healthy person. I know you'll beat it. Everybody else might get it, but not you." When I hear a whiny, complain-y, "I don't feel well" type of thing, I kind of let that go. Instead, I respond to how well they look: "You look wonderful today. You're so healthy. Look at what you can do." In other words, it's reinforcing wellness instead of illness, and I'm refraining from giving my children rewards for being sick. In this way, they are learning to respond with ability, and choose health.

When I was a kid, I was told that if the window was left open, I'd catch a cold. In this foster home I lived in for a few years, many of the children would go around with colds all the time, whether the windows were open or not. I used to say, "But, Mrs. Scarf, I was out all day. We were playing hockey, and the wind was thirty miles an hour. Why would I get a cold because I have the window open? I like to sleep in a room that is nice and cool, with a breeze blowing."

"Well, the cold germs are in the air," she'd say. She also used to tell us that the cold germs were in the linoleum, that if we were to walk across it with our bare feet, the germs would somehow come up through our feet and land in our noses. This seems silly, of course, but many people buy into similar ridiculous notions, especially concerning illness. I no longer do. If I do get a little sniffle or something these days, I treat it as a mistake. I tell no one about it. I'm not interested in having it be a part of my life. I don't think cold thoughts anymore, and I try to reinforce wellness thinking in myself, in my children, and in all the people I deal with.

I don't think of myself as a person who has any special gift other than that I don't want to spend my days being sick. My way of fighting it is to keep myself in shape, which is a very important part of my life. I believe in it strongly for myself and for those who want to make that choice—by simply watching what you eat and not thinking sick and keeping yourself physically active. I truly believe that if you don't take time in your life for exercise and health, then you have to take time later for illness. The choice is yours.

No-Limit Expectations

Once you take responsibility for all aspects of your life, you can go into most any situation and come out smelling like a rose. People will say, "Wow, that guy is so lucky." Or, "She timed that perfectly—it seems like she's always in the right place at the right time." Again, it comes down to attitude. It's an expectation that goes on inside the person who is operating at the highest levels in life, that *Things are going to go well for me.*

Contrast that with people who get in their car and drive to an event, looking for no place to park. It's amazing—when they look for no place to park, they always find no place to park. They're looking straight ahead, with that tunnel vision that typifies most people who are not operating at high levels in their life. What they see is that there are no parking places anywhere. None.

A no-limit person's expectation is, *I've got my own parking place. I know that when I get there, somebody may be using it. I'm not selfish; I don't think that it should be vacant all the time. But now that I'm here, whoever is in my place, I'd like you to get out, please.* Sure enough, they always have a place to park.

I'm telling you that virtually everything in your life boils down to what kinds of attitudes or beliefs you have about any given situation. Let's use the example of having a baby. If you've never had a child before, of course it's going to be a little scary. You'll hear a lot of stories about how it's going to be painful because they're called labor what? *Pains.* And if you go in with the attitude that it's just going to be awful, then sure enough, that's how it will be.

Some people, however, go in and don't even use the word *pain.* They use labor *signals,* as in, *This is a signal for me to use my body in a certain way.* They're so busy and active and participating in this wonderful role and ritual of delivering a child that they don't have time to think pain.

I know it's easy for a man to say this. I've had women tell me, "Look, you can say this all you want, but when you push a watermelon out of your body, then you come back and tell me that it doesn't hurt." I am completely sensitive to that and don't want to diminish anyone's experience, especially as a father of eight. But I genuinely believe in the power of focusing on positive outcomes whenever possible.

It's so important to understand that life is nothing more than a series of choices. I've talked to many young people over the years who have told me that they don't like their science teacher, they don't like their math teacher, they don't get along with their biology teacher, they can't stand this or that. And I ask them, "What are your goals? Why are you going to biology? Are you going there because you have to? You know, you're making the choice to go to school. You could decide not to go if you wanted to. You could become a truant. There are all kinds of options available to you. You're there because you elect to be there—so what do you want out of it?"

Most of them don't want to learn to be a master biologist; they want to get through biology so they don't have to repeat it again and not have a bad time. (And maybe they might even want to learn something too.) So I'll say, "You've got this teacher that you're encountering every day. You think the teacher's goal is to make your life as miserable as possible? That they get up in the morning and say, 'Let's see what I can do for Michael today. I got him yesterday, but I wonder if I can make his life truly miserable today'? If that's your attitude, then you've really got some problems.

"Your goal is to get through biology without having to repeat it, and you're sitting in here talking about how terrible it is. Why not make different choices for yourself that will allow you the option of having a great time in class every day? At the bare minimum, just get through it and make sure that you don't have to do it again. Change your expectations, and respond with ability."

JOURNAL EXERCISE

Imagine it's the weekend, and you're asked to cut the grass. It's a beautiful day, but you suddenly feel so tired that you could sleep for days.

Yet later you're asked, "Hey, would you like to go to this party tonight? I know you said you're tired." I'll bet your response would be, "You bet! I feel great, not tired at all."

When there's something you're really interested in doing, fatigue magically seems to disappear. It's like when you had to do homework in school: you'd sit down and start yawning right away. *I just can't stay awake.* Then you'd get a call from a friend, and you'd spend two hours on the telephone with all the energy in the world.

In your journal, write about how this type of thing has happened before in your life. Then explore how you might choose to react differently to some of the topics discussed in this chapter, expecting only positive outcomes instead.

CHAPTER 4

WHO
YOU REALLY
ARE

One day, I was down in Florida and went out on a friend's boat. While my friend was at the wheel, my eye was drawn to the boat's wake, which is the trail that we were leaving behind. As I was noticing this, I became very aware that the wake didn't drive the boat; it was what we had just experienced. And as I watched it, it completely disappeared. It went for a little ways, and then it was gone.

I realized that there is also a wake that each one of us leaves behind, consisting of everything that has ever come into our lives. This includes all the experiences we've had as well as our beliefs, everything that our parents, our religious training, our schools, and so forth have taught us with the best of intentions.

You have to understand that nothing that constitutes your history is driving the boat called your life, any more than the wake in Florida was driving my friend's boat. What drives your life is the present-moment energy you're generating, not your past. Hanging on to this idea that you have to be the way you've always been because of what has happened to you is as fruitless as believing that the wake drives the boat. You have to let go of that notion.

What I'm talking about here is how to achieve a heightened level of freedom, wherein you move past the ideas that have convinced you that the wake is driving the boat of your life. All those things are nothing more than the trail that you've left behind. In order for you to achieve this freedom that comes with higher awareness, it's important that you erase all those items in the wake. The fact is that you have to let go of the story you've been telling yourself, that what has happened to you in the past forever decides your present.

Six Things You Are Not

If you're not your story, your wake, then what are you? First, I think it's important to look at a few of the things you are not, even though you've probably been told the opposite for your entire life.

1. You are not your name. Most people get so identified and tied in to their name, even though it's only a label. For example, my name is *Wayne,* which means "wagonmaker," and *Dyer,* which is the label of an occupation of people back in England in the 17th century who dyed wool and hides. I am literally a wagonmaker who dyes hides.

Of course, I am not my name at all—it's just something that was given to me to separate me from all the other forms that are on the planet. The same applies to you: you're not your name.

2. You are not your body. I was talking to a man whose son had died, and he was telling me how they had donated his son's body, given the different organs (such as the liver, heart, and eyes) to science. As he was describing this, I was sitting there thinking, *What a nice thing to do, but who was the owner of the body?* When you donate your body parts to science after your death, there is a donator and there is a body being donated. You are the donator; you are not your body. You are that which owns it or notices it or observes it or donates it or whatever you want to call it. You know that. When you say, "This is my arm," the implication is you own something called an arm. Not that you *are* the arm, but you are the owner of it.

3. You are not your mind. Just as you talk about "your" body, you also talk about "your" mind. This implies that you are the owner of the mind. "I was thinking this morning" means that you are the thinker of the thought, the "I" who thinks it. When spiritual teacher Nisargadatta Maharaj was asked if the mind is the true person, he replied, "Examine closely and you will see that the mind is seething with thoughts. It may go blank occasionally, but it does it for a time and reverts to its usual restlessness. A becalmed mind is not a peaceful mind. You say you want to pacify your mind. Is he, who wants to pacify the mind, himself peaceful?"

What a great line this is: *"Is he, who wants to pacify the mind, himself peaceful?"* You, reading this book, want to have a peaceful mind. Is the you who wants to have the peaceful mind yourself peaceful? That's who you are. Again, it's the observer—that's who you are. You are not the thought, you are the *observer* of the thought.

4. You are not your occupation. You're not an engineer or a teacher or a shopkeeper or a secretary or a nurse; such role identification keeps you from your own, true higher self. Again, this is something that you—the Divine, eternal, changeless you; the part of you that always was and always will be—have observed this body of yours doing. To identify yourself by your job means that you're restricting yourself and saying that there are other things that you can't do.

One of the problems so many of us have that keeps us from freedom is that we begin to see ourselves as locked into some occupational title we decided upon many years ago. We believe that's who we are. We can't get past it, even though it's in the wake, the trail that we've left behind. What you have been doing up until now is just that, what you *have been* doing. There's the act of doing it, and then there's the you who's been watching it being done. That's who you are. You're always the witness. You're always the observer who is watching yourself going through the motions. That is, if you place your attention on what you want to be, rather than what you've always done, you can see yourself shifting and being able to do anything.

To that end, I can never think of myself as a teacher or as a writer or as a lecturer or as an anything. When people ask me what it is that I am, I'm always perplexed because I see myself as being able to do an endless number of things, rather than identifying with any particular role.

5. You are not your relationships. You are something that is observing the relationship and someone who is in a relationship, but you are not the relationship itself. This means that when a relationship ends or "fails," it doesn't make *you* a failure. You are uniquely the observer. You are not whom you relate to or are in a particular relationship with at any given moment. It's like a great play that we are all a part of: There are some entrances and some exits. Some people are in for very short parts; some have longer roles to play. You are not any of it.

You have to understand that it's very much like when you go to sleep and have a dream—whatever you need for your dream, whatever characters you happen to require, you create. It isn't who you are; you're simply creating these characters for your dream. Then when you wake up, you don't get mad at the characters for being in your dream. Instead, you know that it was what you needed for that dream. The same thing is true for *this* dream called waking consciousness. Whatever characters you need to act out the play of your life, you create, but that is not who you are. The fact that you are in a relationship with them isn't the definition of you. You are that which is observing it all. You are the witness.

6. **You are not your country, your race, your religion, or any of the other labels that you have placed upon yourself.** You are not an American. You are not black or white or brown. You are not a Christian or a Buddhist. You are that which is eternal. You are a Divine extension of God. You are invisible and eternal and changeless. You may be here in this particular country, practicing this particular religion, or with this particular set of bodily characteristics, but that's not who you are. You are something that is independent of all that, something that is observing it all. There is nothing about you and your racial or ethnic or geographical qualities or characteristics that makes you better than anybody else on this planet who has different racial or ethnic or geographical qualities. You are an extension of God, who just happens to be in this particular kind of body, with these particular practices,

and this body and these practices are nothing more than part of your curriculum from God.

This is the curriculum that you have signed up for, that you are here to learn from. It is merely your method of reaching a higher part of yourself; it is not better than anyone else's. Whether this body is short or tall, dark or light, it comes from your curriculum. Whatever it can or can't do is all in Divine order. As I've said many times, your form is not who you are; it's just a garage where you get to park your soul for a little while.

A good summary to this whole section comes from Nisargadatta Maharaj, whom my dear friend Deepak Chopra introduced me to years ago. Nisargadatta passed on back in the early 1980s, but his work has been very influential in my life.

One of Nisargadatta's students told him, "When I look within, I find sensations and perceptions, thoughts and feelings, desires and fears, memories and expectations. I am immersed in this cloud and I see nothing."

He responded, "That which sees all this and the nothing too is the inner teacher. He alone *is*, all else only appears to be. He is your own Self, your hope and assurance of freedom; find him and cling to him and you will be saved and safe."

"That which sees all this and the nothing too is the inner teacher." It is that which sees these perceptions, feels these sensations, and experiences these thoughts and feelings and desires and fears and memories and expectations. The one who undergoes all that is your inner teacher, and that's who you really are.

No Labels

When I was finishing my doctorate at Wayne State University, I took a course from a professor named Milton Kavinsky, who was one of the best teachers I ever had. I was 1 of 16 students in this advanced seminar in applied metaphysics. Each of us had to take a particular philosophical point of view and present it to the class for two and a half hours, and then Kavinsky would talk about it for an hour. We had to present our points in such a way that it would be applicable, that we'd all be able to say, "When we leave this room today, we will change our life in some way if we can adopt these ideas." This was a required course to get your Ph.D., and it was great.

When it came time for our final exam, Kavinsky told us that it would be 3 hours and 40 minutes, and it would be open book. We could bring any material with us and use as many blue books as we wanted. Some of you may have memories of using those blue books in school, figuring that if you could BS your way through an exam by just filling up the pages, maybe your teacher wouldn't realize that you didn't know what the hell you were talking about. Well, Kavinsky wasn't like that. He could tell instantly if you knew what you were talking about, regardless of how many pages you filled.

The day of the final arrived, and the whole room was filled with the stacks of books we'd all brought with us. Kavinsky passed out our exams at 10 A.M. He said, "You'll have till 1:40 P.M. to write, and you can use anything you want. Now turn over your paper." And then he left the room. On each exam, there were three words and a question mark: *Who are you?* That was it. We were all looking at each other, and then we looked at all the resource material we'd brought with us.

Kavinsky came sauntering back in like Columbo. If you remember the Columbo character from TV, he was always "forgetting" something, but in reality he knew exactly what he was doing. Kavinsky told us, "Oh, I don't know what's the matter with me. . . . I forgot the second sheet. I knew I didn't give my secretary everything. . . ." You know, he's doing this whole routine. In the meantime, we're all sweating.

He passed out this second sheet and said, "Here's a list of all the things that you may not write about. In fact, if you include references to any of these things in your answer, it constitutes a failure of this particular seminar. I don't care about, and you may not write about: your age, your family background, your goals, any of your hobbies, your religious orientation, your voting preferences, your hometown, how much money you've made, or what you think you might ever do in your life." He had about 60 of these things that we were all just getting ready to do our little autobiography on. Then at the bottom of the sheet, he had a quotation from Søren Kierkegaard, the great Danish theologian: "Once you label me, you negate me." Then he left the room for good. I'll tell you, it was one of the most difficult assignments I've ever had, but I've never forgotten it.

It is so hard to define the "unlabelable" part of you, but once you do, it's incredibly powerful. Call it the soul or spirit or whatever—you discover that the invisible part of you really determines everything about your life. You begin to say to yourself, *Okay, how can I apply the awareness of these thoughts and how I use my mind to make my life all that I want it to be, to bring into my life the things that are important to me, to improve the quality of my relationships, to have the success I'm entitled to?* It's about getting to the point where you know that every thought you have has the potential to come into your life. You start to get very cautious about thinking anything that wouldn't work for you, and you begin to question why you would even have such thoughts. You begin to feel a sense of responsibility for everything that goes through your mind.

As You Think, So Shall You Be

As previously mentioned, the ancestor to every action is a thought. Thus, if your mind is focused on what you don't like, then what you don't like has to expand for you. I want to emphasize a very important point here: *Every single problem that you have in your life, you experience in your mind.* You experience it in thought, but it's how you process it that makes something a problem.

If you know that any problem you have in your life is in your mind, then you must know that the solution to any problems also has to be in your mind. The solution can't lie in something or someone outside yourself. If you think someone else makes you miserable, get that person and send them to me—I will treat them, and then you will get better. Of course, that's absurd. We know that the solution as well as the problem is within. Remember, the power is always within you.

You become what you think about all day long. Imagine that you're a salesperson, for example, and you're heading into a meeting with a client. What if your mind, your humanity, your Divineness, your connection to eternity, your total being—which is invisible, but just sort of trapped in this package called Wayne or Joe or Sally—was stuck on a negative thought? If all you can think is, *This isn't going to work out* or *I'm not very good at this* or *I'm not experienced at that* or *This person has been beating around the bush for a long time anyway and they're not going to close on this thing* . . . what are you going to act on? As you think, so shall you be.

That's why it's so important not to clog up your mind with negativity. You can always find something negative if that's what you're looking for. If you want to see an increase in racism in the world, you only have to look around and you'll see it. But if you want to see an increase in brotherhood, you can see that too; you can be part of it. A collective consciousness starts with each one of us.

What you think about expands is the first rule. The second is, *What you think about is already here.* That's really important. In the world of thought, everything you think about is already here—it's not like it's someplace else. Whatever is conceivable in your mind, you can create in form. Boy, do you need to know that . . . and so do your children, especially when they tell themselves there's something they can't do.

When my daughter Sommer was little, I'd lie on my back and lift her up with my arms. With the rest of my kids, I could lift them all the way up and they'd balance themselves, but she couldn't quite get it and would start to fall back. So one day I decided to try something. I began by asking her, "Sommer, what's the name of Daddy's book?"

"You'll See It When You Believe It."

"Well, do you believe?"

"I believe!"

I said, "Come on, I want to hear it. Do you believe?"

"I believe!"

"What do you believe?"

"I can do it!" she said.

Then I went through this whole thing: "Do you see yourself doing it? Can you balance yourself? Do you have the capacity to do that?"

"I can do it, I can do it!"

"All right," I said. And sure enough, when I lifted her up, she balanced herself with no trouble at all. All she had to do was change her thoughts.

Similarly, what do you think the difference is between a child who can swim and one who can't? Do you think that the moment a child knows how to swim, they suddenly have physical capacities they didn't have before? No, they have a new belief and are simply acting on that belief. The same is true of riding a bike or anything like that. It's due to changing around the thought—the physical just sort of adapts to it. Or as the Sufi say, "If you don't have a temple in your heart, you'll never find your heart in a temple." What I'm talking about here is understanding that what you think about expands. Every thought you have is what your humanity is, and every thought you have is already here.

Bringing Thought into Form

When it comes to bringing a thought into form, you must also be willing to do what it takes. You'll notice I didn't say that you have to work hard, you have to struggle, you have to fight, you have to go out there and make it really tough for yourself. The key word in this philosophy is the word *willing*. You must be willing.

Take it from someone who has always been willing to do what it takes. I spent years in an orphanage and in foster homes as a child, and I was the one who was willing to do what it took to make those into pleasant days for myself and all the kids who were there with me, including my older brother. When I wrote *Your Erroneous Zones*, I was told, "We don't have an advertising budget," and "No, we can't send you out on the road," and "No, you can't get on these shows," and so on. Throughout my life, every time somebody told me no, I always thanked them in my heart because that gave me an impetus, spurring on my willingness to do whatever it took to realize my goal.

In the case of *Your Erroneous Zones,* here's what I was willing to do: spend two years of my life selling copies of my book all over the United States. I was told that the only way you could talk to everybody in America was to get on all the big talk shows, but all the big talk shows had never heard of Wayne Dyer. So I found that there's another way to talk to everybody in America—and that's to go to everybody in America. I tried to get on whatever local TV or radio show there was, at places all across the country. At the time, most shows like *AM Columbus* and *Good Morning, Jacksonville* would put you on if you had a new avocado dip. I'd happily appear on these shows, taking copies of my book wherever I went and selling them myself.

I just did whatever I felt I needed to do to get my message out there and didn't tell myself that I had to struggle or that I could ever fail. After all, failure is an editorial judgment imposed by others. Awakened people do not believe in such judgment by others—they listen only to their positive internal messages.

Be an Idealist

You've probably been told that it's idealistic to live your life from the perspective of your higher self. You're told to be realistic about what you can and can't do, and what the limitations of your life have to be. Being an idealist is something that gets criticized a great deal in our culture, with phrases like "You're such a dreamy idealist" meant as an insult.

I love this quotation from William Blake, who is one of my all-time favorite poets: "If the doors of perception were cleansed everything would appear to man as it is, infinite." Can you imagine your reality to be that way, everything infinite? When you cultivate this kind of awareness, your reality is no longer defined by the physical world. This is the kind of reality I'm asking you to examine. It's what I think about all the time. At the very tiniest quantum level, everything is just energy, so in a world where everything is energy and there is no form, that which you observe is what you create. I've always liked what the anthropologist Margaret Mead said: "Never doubt that a small group of thoughtful, committed citizens can change the world; indeed, it's the only thing that ever has." Again, if you can conceive of it in your mind, you can create it in your life.

The corollary of that is if you can't conceive of it in your mind, then you can't create it in your life. In order to be able to create a magnificent, free existence, you must first be able to conceive of it. If you're a realist who says, "I can only go along with what I perceive with my senses, what I can see and hear and touch and taste and smell," then you are destined to be unfulfilled. For example, when I'm about to go onstage and there are thousands of people out there waiting, I do feel nervous. But then I get a picture of myself being able to go out and perform in front of a live audience without any notes, and I'm fine.

When my daughter Skye was 12, she was preparing to sing before a large crowd for the first time. It was a really exciting, exquisite time for her, but she felt afraid. So I asked her, "I know you're excited and nervous, but can you see yourself singing?"

She said, "Yeah, I really can."

"Then all you have to do is have that picture. The rest of it, all the details, will get handled," I assured her. And everything turned out wonderfully for her.

If you say things like, "But I've never done this before. This is a brand-new thing for me, so I'm not going to be very good at it. I'm going to probably fall down or forget my lines," you become that realist who says, "I'm only human." You put in all kinds of limitations, and that becomes the very blueprint you rely on for your life.

You don't want to be the architect who relies upon a limited blueprint. You want to say, "Yes, I'm an idealist. Of course I believe that world peace is possible." What are we going to do instead—create a world where we don't have nuclear weapons and we're all at peace with people who believe that it's impossible? How is that ever going to work? We have to have idealists.

Thomas Edison was an idealist: "Yeah, we can light the world." Alexander Graham Bell was an idealist: "Of course we can communicate with each other over telephones." If you're a realist, you are that which is being told over and over again, "These are your limitations." Remember that who you are is the observer, the Divine witness. You are the one who is watching all this transpire, knowing that there are no limits and no boundaries upon the path of enlightenment.

In order to become an idealist, you must first trust your intuition. Quietly affirm that you will define your own reality from now on, that your definition will be based on your own inner wisdom. When you come to trust in yourself, you're trusting in the very wisdom that created you. Your intuition is an incredibly powerful thing. When you allow it to be the ruling force in your life, you remove all that "realistic" pessimism that holds and confines and restrains you.

In my book *Everyday Wisdom*, I say that "If prayer is you talking to God, then intuition is God talking to you." This intuitive knowing, this inner motivation, this directional push in certain ways, is really God talking to you. When you ignore that intuition, you pay quite a price.

We've all had instances of ignoring our intuition, when we later say, "I knew I should have said no. I knew I shouldn't have done that," leaving us to deal with a negative, ego-driven attitude. But sooner or later, we find ourselves getting to the point where we don't ignore our intuition any longer. We begin to have a collaboration with God rather than fighting it.

Think about something that you once believed in before you were told it was impossible. I can remember, for example, believing at one time that I was really terrific at drawing. Then when I was in the fourth grade, a teacher came up to me and said, "That's the worst drawing I've ever seen. You're not good at that." To this day, many years later, I still carry around some silly notion about what someone told me when I was in the fourth grade regarding my ability to draw.

Go through all the things that you have come to believe, maybe religious beliefs that you have had handed to you or things that you've read or been taught that really influenced you, which are now causing you to admit, "Maybe this caused me to have too closed of a mind." Begin to examine them and say, "Nothing has to be impossible for me today. I'm going to let go of all those ancient ideas." If you made a list, you could probably find 100 of those things to systematically cross off, as you realize they no longer need to drive your boat or influence you today.

Then I'd like you to practice experimenting with your new reality. Keep a vision of what you want to occur, or someone you want to meet—anything that is important to you. Focus on it manifesting in your own life. Keep track of all the little things that lead up to bringing it about. After a while, you're going to note that your reality has become one in which you play a role as co-creator. It may take you a while to become more idealistic about your ability to create the kind of being that you want to be and to see what you want appearing in your life, but it will happen as you keep that inner vision front and center.

JOURNAL EXERCISE

Try the assignment I was given by Milton Kavinsky: Find a time when you can set aside three and a half hours, and see what happens when you write in your journal for that length of time about who you are, without using any labels. What does this exercise help you see? And how can you bring that powerful presence to the forefront in your life, so you can more effectively manifest your desires into form?

PART II

TRUE
SUCCESS

Success is not the key to happiness.
Happiness is the key to success.
If you love what you are doing,
you will be successful.

— Albert Schweitzer

CHAPTER 5

CONSULT YOUR INNER SIGNALS

The idea of success is so often tied to happiness in people's minds. It's true that they are both inner concepts—something that you are. When you have success inside you, you bring it to every single thing you do in life. You bring it to your children; you don't get it from raising them the "right" way. You don't get it by closing the deal; you bring it to every aspect of the deal. You don't get it by concerning yourself with your commission or quotas; you get it by concentrating on your customers. You forget about all the things you're going to obtain, and instead enjoy what you discover along the path of enlightenment. If you simply go out and endeavor to live your own life the way you choose, making every day a miracle, success will arrive in your life in amounts greater than you could ever have anticipated.

There's a nice parable that illustrates what I'm talking about here: An old cat and a little kitten are in an alley. The kitten is chasing its tail, and the cat comes up and asks, "What on earth are you doing?"

The kitten says, "I have been to cat philosophy school, and I learned that there are two things in the world that are important for a cat: The first is that happiness is the most important thing. The second is that happiness is located in our tails. So, what I figured out is that if I chase and chase my tail until I finally get a hold of it, I will have a lock on eternal happiness."

The old cat replies, "You know, I haven't had the opportunity to go to cat philosophy school like you. I've wandered around the alleys all my life. But it's really amazing, I've learned the same things you have. I know that the most important thing for a cat is happiness and, indeed, that it is located in my tail. The only difference between you and me is I've discovered that if you go about your business and do the things that are important to you, happiness will follow after you wherever you go."

The same is true of success.

As I've said, self-defeating people are externally motivated. When it comes to success, they again look outside themselves, to acquisitions, achievements, or the like. Internally motivated people, however, do what is right for them, and as long as it doesn't involve hurting somebody else, it's okay. Success is something that's found within themselves.

The internally motivated person is someone who is willing to suffer some outrage and stand up to established authority, whenever necessary, in order to get the things that they want or believe to be important. Being that kind of person stems from consulting what I call your "inner signals." *You* make the choices; you follow your own guidance at all times. You don't look to other people or external factors to show you the way.

Opinions, Reputation, and Character

When it comes to what other people think, it's important to understand that their opinions are just that—they're not necessarily the best ideas or even the truth, at least not *your* truth. They're not necessarily anything other than another person's judgment.

Opinions are of very little value by themselves. It is only what we do with them that makes any difference in the world. So what I have learned to do with other people's opinions is to remember that they can't hurt me, they can't destroy me, they can't make me into anything less than I am as a human being.

Like opinions, reputation is a meaningless concept. Let's say I go out and speak to a thousand people—well, there are a thousand opinions out there. They are all unique and different from one another, and I don't know what any of them are. This is what supposedly constitutes my reputation. I have a thousand reputations going, and I have no control over what any one person decides they're going to do with what I say. My reputation is not in my hands, but located in other people's opinions.

Terry Cole-Whittaker wrote a book that has one of the greatest titles I have ever seen: *What You Think of Me Is None of My Business.* I couldn't agree more. I don't care about my reputation. I'm not interested in it at all. Since it's external, located in other people exclusively, it doesn't really pertain to me. Whatever I do, at whatever level I'm doing it—whether I'm onstage at Carnegie Hall or sitting with a friend of mine—what other people think of me is about them and where they are.

I was a guest on *The Tonight Show* many times, and every time I appeared, I got letters from viewers. I'd tell a joke or say a funny little remark, and it would inspire 50 people

73

to write me about it. Some would say, "That was a funny joke. That was really terrific, you were sensational." Others would say, "How dare you make a joke like that? That's not a funny thing to say at all." And still others would say, "I didn't think what you said was appropriate. It was in bad taste." Even though these letters were all different, they were all about my reputation, and none of them had anything to do with me. I was telling a joke; I don't know what the viewers were doing.

I've learned not to be concerned with my reputation but instead be concerned with my character. That is internal, and I'm always in charge of that. I can never be in charge of how other people are going to perceive me, because that's their opinion and they're entitled to it. Again, I can't control that. The only thing I can control is my character, which comes from my thoughts and the love I have inside, not my reputation and what other people think of me.

I once received two letters about one of my books. One of the letters said it was the greatest thing the writer had ever read, that it had changed his life completely. He gave me all this credit for the transformation that had taken place in his life as a result of reading it. On the same day, in the same mail, was a letter from somebody who thought the very same book was so bad that he wanted a refund for it. So here's what I did: I sent a copy of the really nice letter to the guy who had written me the angry one, and I sent the negative one to the guy who had written the positive one. I included a note that said, "You may be right"—not "I'm right and you're wrong"—and signed my name.

Examples like this show you how silly it is to go around being consumed by what other people think. What other people think is just that, and if you live your life by such external motivation, you will never enjoy true success.

Hidden Opportunities

Suppose you took somebody else's advice, and it didn't work out for you. Rather than being disappointed and playing the blame game, try reframing your thinking and accepting responsibility for your choices. For example, if I have a stockbroker who gives me advice to buy a stock and it goes down, it wasn't his advice that made me buy the stock—it was *my own* advice. I took his opinion and said to myself, *I would like to make some fast money on buying this stock. He says it will go up, and I'm believing it. I'm buying it; it's my decision.* I can't blame him if the stock goes down. I might feel I need to get a different stockbroker, but I take responsibility for the losses I've encountered.

Everything that happens to you that is considered negative, such as failure or loss, in fact contains a hidden opportunity for empowerment. The seeds for all solutions to all problems are in the problems themselves. The cure is always in the illness: A cold has within it the opportunity to transcend that virus. Alcoholism has within it the seeds for transcending something about yourself that was controlling you before. That is why the first thing reformed alcoholics often do is celebrate their alcoholism, saying, "It was the greatest thing that ever happened to me. Getting help saved my life."

You ought to be the most grateful to the people or circumstances that you feel are causing you the most upset in your life, because they're the ones who are forcing you to take a good look at yourself. It isn't what you face that controls you, since you have dealt with it and moved on. It's what you *don't* face that controls you: The overweight person who won't face his compulsive eating. The workaholic who won't face the fact that she's working too much. The people in a relationship who won't face the trouble between them.

If you can't say no within a relationship, you'll have to say no to the relationship itself eventually. What I mean by this is that you need to draw boundaries with other people, including the ones who love you the most, such as your partner, your children, your other family members, your friends, and so on. You must let them know you have to be your own person, and when they want you to be something you can't be—because it conflicts with where you are on your path of enlightenment—you'll have to say no. You'll need to speak up for yourself: "No, I can't do that. I can't be your little victim. I can't be your servant. I can't be the kind of person you try to control, telling me when I have to be somewhere or what I have to think." Believe it or not, this will actually strengthen your relationships.

No is a big word to be able to say. You can do it with love and dignity and respect, as well as firmness and commitment. Don't say, "You're controlling me." Instead, highlight the commitment you're making: "I have to say no to these things that you want of me because I can't be what you think I should be." Then you'll never have to say no to the relationship itself because it will flourish and grow. Again, it's only the things you don't face—the ones you continue to ignore, hoping they'll go away—that are really controlling your life in a negative way. Setting boundaries helps you reverse all that so you can stand up for yourself no matter what, be it to the people who love you the most or the ones who don't even know you.

Imagine you're being treated poorly by a sales clerk. You can say no within that relationship as well: "No, I won't be treated this way. I think you're great, but I won't be talked to this way. I'm going to get my refund," or whatever the case may be. You don't have to walk away in a huff and lose out on what you want. You have to be able to act with an inner conviction, with the love that you *are*.

You know that what's inside of you is a result of what you think. Teach yourself to expect positive outcomes in all your encounters, processing your world in such a way that when you encounter a situation in which people are having a different opinion than you are, you take the opportunity to respond with what you have inside, and that's always love.

You can't give away what you don't have. If you don't have love for yourself, then you can't be loving to others. Therefore, self-love is the name of the game. And it has nothing to do with conceit. A lot of people confuse that, assuming that if you love yourself, then you must be conceited. Understand that being conceited is just another form of externally motivated approval seeking. If you have to tell others how great you are in order for you to feel good about yourself, then their opinion of you is what is controlling you. It's like you're giving up your personal power in order for others to like you, and that is not self-loving in the slightest.

The no-limit person has what I call a "quiet love affair" with themselves. If you asked them, "Do you love yourself?" they'd respond, "Of course I do. It's what I am. I mean, why wouldn't I love what I am?" Because self-love is already a given. This person is so busy being, so focused on what they're about and what they're here for, that they don't even notice what their neighbors are doing or what everybody else is saying about them. They certainly don't blame anybody for anything that happens in their life—they only consult their inner signals, which always come from love.

Networking with Love

Keep in mind that the universal force of love is there for each one of us all the time. No matter who you are, where you are, what the conditions of your life are—whether you live inside a mansion or a prison or are homeless—it doesn't make any difference. You are Divine. You are part of the Divineness and perfection of the universe. If you try tapping into that, I bet you will see really dramatic shifts take place in your life. I cannot guarantee that this will work for you, of course. All I know is that all the people I've heard about who have tried the love route discovered that what were problems before are no longer there.

Let's think about what would happen if we brought the universal force of love to our business culture. As it is now, the power structure generally goes from top to bottom and flows downward—it starts at the top with the boss, goes down to the vice presidents, and then to the assistant vice presidents, and so on, all the way down to the clerks and interns. The purpose of power here is to get as much of it as possible, so people are constantly collecting it so they can move up this ladder and get to "the top." But there's another organizational flow chart that operates in the universe, called *networking,* and it is about love. Here, every single person is about giving power away, not collecting it. Everybody is working toward the same goal: to help everybody else within the organization. Nobody wants any power here. It's like as soon as you give somebody any power, they say, "No, that's not for me," and they pass it on.

Networking is an outstanding way to get anything done. It's almost like a word-of-mouth approach to living: if you have an idea, you give it away freely to somebody else, then they take it and pass it on to somebody else, and on and on. That process of pushing it out can influence the entire world, so try to network all the time with everyone. Rather than trying to collect power, getting someone else to do something for you, or organizing others so they are in a linear fashion either above or below you, see everybody as equal and able to contribute. That's how I see myself.

Every time I give a book away, I feel like I'm networking. As I've mentioned, I'm not doing any of this for money—I love doing what I do and making a difference in people's lives. Whenever I speak to an organization, I ask, "Will you be taping it?" They often get very nervous about it and say, "Well, we were thinking about it, but weren't sure about the cost." I reply, "Why don't you just get a tape recorder, and you can make what I say available for all the people in your organization as a training device? It won't cost anything and doesn't have to be a big production." In these cases, all I can think of is how terrific it is to network—if you're authentic and talking about something that is good and beautiful and will help people improve the quality of their lives, then you want as many people as possible to hear it.

It's really a win-win situation, as I feel that whenever someone hears a recording of me and passes it on to somebody else, there's a very good chance that this person will say, "Hey, that's really good! I think I'll go get his books." Even though that's not my purpose in doing it, it will all come back tenfold.

Of course everybody has to make a living, and there's nothing wrong with that. Everyone who produces my products, from the editors to the marketing folks to the people who design and package them to the warehouse staff, is going to make something out of it. But every single time they disseminate one of my products, they're also participating in this networking, because somebody's life is going to be improved, and they'll tell somebody else about it, and on and on it goes.

That's how networking works. You don't think of yourself; you give it all away. Yet the more you give away, the more you get back. It's important to note here that if you're only giving something away in order to get something back for yourself, then you will never have enough. You'll always be looking for more because you're stuck in the mind-set of lack. If you know you already have enough, and you appreciate it very much, then, paradoxically, more will keep coming to you in your life.

That's really what enlightenment or higher consciousness is: *What I have is enough. I have everything I need to enjoy total, complete peace and happiness right now. Anything else I get back is just a bonus.* That's what networking is, and you can network with love all the time.

Your Value and Worth

Your value does not come from what you accomplish. Your worth as a human being is not determined by whether you win or not. If you have to win to order to have value, then somebody else has to lose, and that somebody else who's losing is determining whether you're a winner or not. If they don't cooperate, then you're the loser.

When you're always looking over your shoulder to determine whether you're worthy or not, you're giving your value up as a person and putting it in the hands of someone else who you hope won't make as much money as you or have as many clients as you do. Don't you understand that those external motivations are now controlling your life? If someone lands one more account than you do, that makes you a loser? No.

You are what you believe about yourself. Your value doesn't come from anything but what you choose to think, and you contain the willingness and the ability to think anything you want. That's yours. No one can take that away from you. You can always think what you want, in the way that you choose. So rather than continuing to be externally directed, learn to listen only to yourself when it comes to how your life is going to be run. This is nothing to do with abusing anybody else, wishing other people ill will, stepping on anybody else, or anything like that.

The most important thing to learn in life is a sense of appreciation for yourself. It's very important for you to realize that you are at once unique and also part of the entire universe. That is, we are all related in some ways to each other—if one of us is starving on this planet, then all of us are starving—yet you are still special in the world. You must get to the point that you can fuse that dichotomy, saying to yourself, *I am at once male and female. I am at once capable of doing what a man and a woman can do, so therefore I don't have to be concerned about whether I'm doing something that's feminine or masculine. I can be gentle; I can cry. In my position of rightness about what I believe, there's also room for hearing what somebody else has to say and even being willing to change that. In my position of being special and unique, there's also lots of room to be part of all of humankind.*

Understand that as you sit here right now, no one has ever thought what you are thinking. No one has ever occupied the space you occupy. Really try to comprehend what philosophers call "the existential aloneness"—that you are alone in the universe, and you must experience that aloneness in such a way that you never allow yourself to feel down or depressed by it. Nobody can ever get behind your eyeballs and feel what you feel and experience what you experience, except for you. You can be in a room full of people and still be alone. You could be making love to the person you adore more than anything in the world, and you're still alone. You are always experiencing things in your own unique and special way.

In all of time, no one can ever get to an understanding of themselves, of the universe, of what it means to be a no-limit person, unless they get to this point called inner peace—and that is something you can never obtain but can only feel inside. Learning to tune in to your own specialness and consult your inner signals will help point the way to lasting and genuine success.

JOURNAL EXERCISE

What has represented success to you so far: Is it a nice house, a large salary, a closetful of clothes, or being the first one to have the latest gadget? Go ahead and write these down in your journal. Then take a few minutes to envision a new, internally motivated version of success. What might it look like if you weren't the kitten chasing its tail? Write that down as well, and see which version truly resonates with you now.

CHAPTER 6

BE A YAYSAYER, NOT A NAYSAYER

Not long ago, a dear friend of mine found out that he had a severe kind of cancer for a man his age. After sharing the diagnosis, the doctor told him, "You have 15 seconds to make up your mind about whether this cancer is going to defeat you or you're going to defeat it. You have 15 seconds. If you believe something like, *It's impossible. I can't do it. It's not fair*; if you get yourself all worked up; if you're upset about it and tell yourself that this shouldn't have happened and *Why me?* then you are going to be one more victim.

"But if you can somehow get inside your head the idea that you have a chance to do something about this, and it may be one of the biggest tests of your life, then you're going to have a chance to beat this thing."

My friend instantly decided that he was going to defeat it—and that's exactly what he did. Whenever I think about this moving story, I'm reminded that within all of us lies the capacity to do the most tremendous things.

The brain is an incredible instrument. Yes, that thing we carry between our ears every day is so vast and immense in its scope, composed of *trillions* of cells. It has the ability to make billions upon billions of decisions, to store facts and experiences in a memory bank that lasts a lifetime. It has the ability to learn and remember how to calculate and speak multiple languages and do most anything we want it to do. In fact, it was once estimated that if we were to try to reproduce one human brain and all of its abilities in a computer, it would take a piece of land the size of the state of Texas in order to house that machine. Imagine that. Have you ever driven across Texas? It takes a full day of going 70 miles an hour to cross from one side to the other. That's a big piece of land, and it really illustrates what the human brain is capable of.

You've got this fantastic computer, but how much of it do you use? If you're lucky, maybe a neighborhood in El Paso. And how much do you give it credit for being able to do what it does? It can do anything. It's your will. It's your life. It's all there in that computer, which you only use a fragment of. It's time to change that.

I often wonder why so many of us ignore our inherent capability for greatness and allow ourselves to get bogged down by daily living. I think it has to do with a breeding of negativity; people are simply looking for things to be down about. For example, I've never had an unemployment thought in my life. I can think of the stories I heard in my own family about the Great Depression, and many folks I've talked to had a very hard time during that era but figured out a way to make it through. I like to focus on what we're capable of, even though I've had lots of people over the years try to teach me about how limited we supposedly are. I don't believe it.

I have found that the highest-level individuals I've ever met are what I call *"yay*sayers,"or people who like the world and everything in it. And just like using more of our brains, we can learn to say yes to most anything in life.

One-Baggers versus Two-Baggers

When I was a young man, I worked as a bag boy for many years. To this day, I watch their technique whenever I go into a grocery store. As I stand in line, I'll invariably see what I call the "one-bagger." This is the guy who opens the bag gingerly, picks up a can of peas, studies it, and places it in the bag. In the meantime, the counter where the groceries are coming through is getting completely backed up. The cashier has to stop her job, which is to take the money, and assist this guy in *his* job. It's almost as if his attitude is, *There's no cashier in the world that I can't make stop and help me.* It makes no difference to him, after all. He works at one pace—*slow*—and his attitude is one of indifference, which is also his approach to life.

Then I'll notice the other bag boy, whom I call the "two-bagger." He's the guy who's got two cashiers that he's bagging for. He's going back and forth, but he's cheerful to all the customers, asking how they're doing and so forth. All the while, he's bagging quickly and efficiently—he's not crushing the eggs or the bread. He'll fill the bag and set it down in the customer's cart, and then he'll do the same for the next cashier, and then come back to the first one. It's like he's got a contest going with himself.

I always was a two-bagger, and I still am. In fact, I won't let anyone ever touch my groceries. I want them bagged my way, I want them bagged now, and I don't want to stand there and wait for somebody, hoping that life will get better for him before he can get through with my groceries. I used to think of myself as the world-champion bag boy, and there were no two cashiers in the world who could keep up with me. Sometimes I'd even challenge the three fastest ones, telling them, "I can bag for all three of you all day, and not one of your customers will ever have to pick up a bag."

I'm telling you right now that I can predict what the first bag boy's life is going to be like: He's going to be a self-defeating one-bagger all his life. He will go through life literally staying a bag boy, or becoming something equivalent, and he is going to go home and tell his wife how rotten it was that he was passed over for a promotion, and the boss doesn't really like him, and he didn't get the raise everybody else got, and everybody discriminates against him, and it isn't fair, and how dare they do this sort of thing to him! He's going to be very unfulfilled, and he's going to be an expert at being right.

He will be right in what he is and what he says, because he will convince himself that *Everybody and everything else out there is the reason why I am the way I am. It has nothing to do with me or my attitude toward my job and what I do. There's a conspiracy out there to keep me from getting ahead. They just don't want me to make it.* Sadly, one-baggers rarely change. They typically do not understand how to respond with ability to life in order to make different, better choices.

The two-bagger, on the other hand, will probably go on to own four or five chains of grocery stores. At the very least, he will never allow himself to be defeated; he'll go through his life with a growth mind-set, trying all kinds of things. There will be no such thing as unemployment for him—no matter what happens to the economy, he won't allow that to happen to him. If he were laid off tomorrow, he's the kind of guy who would go out and apply for 100 jobs. If he got 100 rejections, he'd apply for 100 more, and he'd keep doing it and doing it until he got the kind of position he wants. He's the rare kind of person who will make his own opportunities.

Now, how do you explain the difference between these baggers? This is one of the things that mystifies so many people. Here you have two individuals who seem the same on the surface—they have the same pay, the same number of coffee breaks during the day, the same age and background—so how do you explain one of them being a one-bagger and one of them being a two-bagger? Where does it come from? Is it opportunity, talent, or education? No, it has nothing to do with any of that, or with the types of things that social scientists are always looking for.

The difference is related to perseverance, drive, and pride in oneself—if someone has those qualities, it doesn't matter what they do. Two-baggers are simply internally motivated, operating with a sense of peace and serenity.

You see, paying your bills and getting a nice job and having a family are all great things, but they are not the avenue to inner peace. If you're looking for peace in what somebody else is doing, including your own children, or if you're looking for peace because you do what you're supposed to and have a nice nest egg, you're going to always be looking outside yourself for the source of your fulfillment. Until you look within yourself, you'll never find it; it is never going to be there.

There has to be a whole new set of rules to help you get along, to make life a little easier and more pleasant. The old rules teach you to be happy by focusing on the externals, such as pleasing other people or doing what others tell you to do. If you want inner peace, you have to do the opposite: You need to consult and please yourself, and you cannot be cautious. You've got to be a yaysayer.

The Yaysayer's Guide to Success

Self-defeating, naysaying people have a great fear of the unknown. They are afraid of doing anything different, of wandering into territory they've never been before. They want to be safe. They don't want to take risks. They whine and complain about anything that represents change, which is so frightening to them. They are afraid of new ideas, and work very hard to stay only with the familiar.

Naysayers are loaded with prejudices that are most often not based on anything in reality. Instead, they cling to the idea of, *If I don't know somebody out there, or if something is new, I reject it immediately because it's frightening to me.* Again, it comes back to fear of the unknown. They won't try out a new town, even if there's great opportunity there. They won't make a career change at a certain time in their life because it's too frightening or they might fail. Rather than face the prospect of failing, they just keep to the familiar. They do this in their relationships, with their friends, and even in the kinds of restaurants they go to. They eat in the same places, having their meat cooked the same way over and over again, and never trying an unfamiliar cuisine—not because they don't like it, but because the unknown simply represents something to stay away from.

Most people accept the unknown and aren't intimidated or immobilized by it. When change comes along, they deal with it effectively and don't let themselves become depressed by it. They'll occasionally try something new, but their circle of friends tends to think and act and behave in the same kinds of ways that they do. They tend to associate with like-minded people who enjoy the same activities. Maybe they all like to play mah-jongg or go rock climbing, or maybe they all like the same kinds of books and movies.

There's nothing wrong with enjoying people who have the same interests. However, with it can come a kind of acceptance of, *My friends are people I share things in common with. Those are the kinds of friends I have.* I'm not putting it down; rather, I want to illustrate the difference between most people, who are open and accepting, and the self-defeating folks who are really afraid.

Then there's the no-limit yaysayer, who welcomes the unknown. In fact, they seem so excited by it that they even seek it out. This person doesn't require an agenda—they don't need to have a plan or a lot of goals or specific items that they must know in advance about how things are going to work out. They're not intimidated by anyone because they don't have that quality of prejudice. They don't prejudge anyone or anything. They have an open mind about things, and no prejudice whatsoever.

The self-defeating person would never dream of trying to learn a foreign language, for instance. They'll say things like, "The reason I can't speak a foreign language is because I didn't get it in high school." They forget that they could have 60 or 70 years ahead of them to do anything they want to, including learning a new language.

At age 90, the awakened person will see a list of foreign-language classes and say, "I think I'd like to learn Spanish. I've never spoken it before." And they'll sign up and try something new.

Here's another story that illustrates the difference between these two types of people: Two guys walk into a new deli. The waiter hands them the menu, which says that the specialty of the house is tongue sandwiches.

One fellow looks at the menu and says, "Tongue! That's disgusting."

The other fellow looks at it and says, "Tongue. Hmm . . . never had it before. I'll have a double tongue sandwich!"

The first fellow goes, "Blech. You are disgusting. How can you eat tongue? It makes me sick just thinking about it. I don't see how a civilized person could ever eat something like that."

The waiter says, "You don't have to eat it. You can have anything else. What'll you have?"

"I'll have what I always have: an egg-salad sandwich, heavy on the mayonnaise."

As Albert Einstein, who was a person who wandered into the mysterious and the unknown all the time, once said, "The most beautiful thing we can experience is the mysterious." Imagine if we depended on self-defeating people to move progress forward when we know it involves exploring the unknown. Think about them being back in the age of the explorers, saying, "Uh-uh. You're not fooling me. I'm not leaving here in any boat and dropping off the edge of the earth." What if there hadn't been some people who said, "Maybe there isn't an edge to the earth—let's go find out"?

You see, progress cannot happen if you always do things the way you've always done them. As long as you are willing to stay as you are or to stick with the familiar or never try out anything new, then it is by definition impossible to grow.

No-limit people are excited by the unknown. How do you become such a yaysayer? Maybe go on a trip without a map. When you get to a hotel and they don't have any place to sleep, go on to someplace else. Or sleep in the car or out under the stars. Or just go west—that is, every time you make a turn, be sure you're going west. Some of you might be thinking, *What, is he crazy?* But try it, knowing that wherever you end up is going to be okay.

Walk barefoot in the park, or make love on the beach. Whatever it may be, be sure that you're doing something different from the way you've always done it. Change up your vacations; don't go back to the same place you've always gone to every year for the last 20 years and stay in the same room, the same bed.

Some people run their whole lives avoiding the unknown. While they feel right in their own minds, they don't have a sense of inner peace. And they'll never have it if they're not willing to try new things.

The Importance of Internal Motivation

What do you think a no-limit person would do if they arrived at a party and found out that everybody had dressed formally while they'd dressed casually? They wouldn't even notice. They're not focused on external appearances, on what other people are wearing or how they look; they understand that dressing is just something that you do. You do it based on what you feel like wearing. Now, this is not to say that this person is going to show up at a formal affair in tennis shoes and a loincloth. After all, that would be a person who is still trying to impress other people with their uniqueness—other people's impressions are continuing to control them.

Internal motivation is the important concept here. No-limit people don't dress based on what other people are going to say or think or feel or do, or how other people are attired; they dress based on what seems to make sense for them. When they arrive someplace, they don't say, "Oh my God, you've got jeans on and I don't," or "Oh, I've got to go home and change so I can be like everybody else." Someone would have to point that out to them, because they won't notice.

That's very different from what you'll hear so-called experts talking about, about how imperative it is to be concerned about everything you wear: they say it's so important that if you don't have the right outfit, you shouldn't even bother going out!

I've never found that things like this have had much of an effect in my life. I mean, if I show up someplace and everybody else is dressed differently, nobody cares. I enjoy my meal just as much, and that's the end of it. It's the concept of not noticing that's really crucial in this whole area of living at the highest level.

Remember, when you are looking for love, it will always elude you. When you're looking for happiness, it will always elude you. When you *become* those things, however, they're just there. You don't have them, they have you. What we have to do to understand this business of self-love or self-acceptance is to really get the notion that what you're here for and what you're doing is something that finds you. It isn't something that you find.

Your thought processes create the images that you have. Those images create your behavior, and you can't back one up from the other unless you're willing to think it's going to work out, and that's the premise you're operating from. That's a very important point if you want to be enlightened. If you believe it's going to work out, then you'll start to see opportunities. If you don't, then you'll see obstacles.

I've never believed that people who work hard and do all the right things make a lot of money, and then become successful. I think it's the other way around—I think successful people make a lot of money at whatever they do, and make a lot of friends and all that, because the successful person is someone who has it within them. Again, it is what they are.

JOURNAL EXERCISE

In your journal, write down some ways you've been a naysayer in life. What have you always wanted to do but been afraid to? Next, write about what would happen if you didn't let fear hold you back but said yes to what your heart really wants. Try going out there and becoming a yaysayer!

CHAPTER 7

MODELS OF ENLIGHTENMENT

When I was living in New York, we'd go to Jones Beach when it opened on Memorial Day. We'd arrive on what was sure to be a hot day, as it often got up to 90 degrees on Long Island at the end of May. Now, if you want to see who most exemplifies no-limit people, look no further than the little children who had been locked up in their houses all winter. They knew this was the only water they were going to get to play in. If they didn't take advantage of it, the closest they'd get would be the bathtub back home, like it had been all winter long.

The parents, on the other hand, would focus on the temperature of the water. *There was ice in it just 30 days ago,* they'd think. *That's going to be some cold water.* They'd get there and obsess about that cold water, even though it was 85 degrees out, as they sat around and got their picnics together or what have you. The children would zoom right into the water and wouldn't even notice that it was cold. Even if they got a little blue, they didn't care. They were in the water, at the beach, and it was fun and exciting for them. They didn't tell themselves how awful it was going to be, or even think cold thoughts. They were having the best time!

The parents were supposedly there to have a good time too, but here's how they'd talk: "Look at those kids, swimming in the water when it's still May. I can't believe how crazy they are." But who was crazy? The children were free and spirited and enjoying themselves, while the parents' narrative kept them from being able to enjoy that day, that moment, that special set of circumstances.

Children instinctively know the power of a good attitude. They know that if you expect to enjoy a fun day at the beach, then that's exactly what you will do. You can capture the spirit of unspoiled, creatively alive, excited-about-everything children even now, simply by allowing that little boy or girl inside of you to come out.

It's Never Too Late to Have a Happy Childhood

I understand that the concept of letting out your "inner child" may be uncomfortable for some people. If you didn't have the happiest of childhoods, then I suggest you try to understand that your sense of self takes over even when you're very young. If you're an adult now, it's time to stop blaming your parents for what you could or couldn't do, or what you're able or not able to do in life. I was a teacher for many years, and I know that you cannot teach English literature or algebra to someone who doesn't want to learn it, who flat-out refuses to. No one can take away a person's childhood unless they are an outright abuser, which is a different subject altogether and not what I'm talking about here.

If you feel that your parents kept you from doing the things you wanted to do as a kid, it's time to start responding with ability. As I used to tell my clients, "You didn't know how to deal effectively with your father back then. You didn't know how to get what you felt you were entitled to from your mother or from your grandparents or whatever. I understand that you were small and they were large and they set the rules and all that. The time has come for you to take responsibility for how you reacted to your parents."

Yet many people just want to look for fault. They go to their therapist, they talk to their friends, and they come up with all the reasons why things aren't going well for them. I found out in working with people that almost everyone is looking for excuses, rather than taking responsibility for their own lives. To my clients, I insisted, "Even when you were a child, you were making choices. There might have been 50 people exposed to one kind of teacher in a school, and there are always some children who make different choices about the way they reacted to that teacher than others did. There are always some kids who somehow knew not to be manipulated, feel victimized, or be pushed around, and they would stand up for what they believed early in their lives. Those were choices. You may not have known how to make other choices at that time, or maybe you were too afraid or you weren't encouraged to or whatever, but that's what it really was about: taking responsibility for what you are as a human being and applying it throughout your life."

I've known many families with several children, and some of those children are able to figure out how to have a happy childhood, no matter what. Even in a situation that other people would construe as negative, where others would be beaten down by their situation and feel that somebody else controlled them, they were able to thrive. I know this subject intimately, having spent much of my childhood in foster homes and an orphanage, never knowing my father. But I didn't let circumstances bring me down, and I have had a fantastic life. There is nothing special about me, though—anyone can stop focusing on the past, on the wake of the boat.

I think it's important to go back through your whole life and take ownership for how you reacted. This is not to say that the influence of a parent isn't important and can't have a significant effect on a child. But it doesn't do you any good to look back with blame—you must look at your past with responsibility. You can then shift your attitude to having a wonderful present.

It's never too late to have a happy childhood. Never! If you didn't like your childhood, fix it now. "I didn't get to go to any amusement parks," you might say. Well, many of them are still around. "I'm sixty-eight years old." If you want to go to an amusement park and be three years old, that's not going to happen. Yet there's nothing to stop you from visiting an amusement park at your age now. They're open. They'll let you in if you have the entrance fee. You can do anything you want. That's a very important concept.

I had one client tell me, "My mother would never let me ride a bicycle. She would never let me roll down a hill or get dirty."

I said, "I see. Okay, there's a hill over there with some dirt, and there are bicycles over here. You can essentially have anything now that you wanted back then."

"I didn't come here and pay you to teach me how to ride a bicycle!"

I said, "I'm just trying to get you to understand that the only reason you don't know how to ride a bicycle is because you've never gotten on one and actually gone through the trial and error that goes with learning anything. Stop blaming your mother for the fact that you couldn't stand up to her throughout your life, and go ahead and do it anyway. If my mother or any adult in my life would have told me that I couldn't ride a bicycle when I was a kid, there's no possibility that I would have paid very much attention to that. Yet you did, for some reason. That's where you were, whereas I was able to get on a bicycle and make it happen."

You take responsibility for your life and your choices, always. When you learn to respond with ability, you don't have to spend endless hours in therapy, going through deep analysis to figure out why you were toilet trained harshly or why your mother liked your sister better or any of those kinds of things that you hear people using as excuses for why they're not where they want to be in their life.

It isn't doing you any good to toss out a lot of blame for your parents and focus on things like, "Oh, they're old-fashioned," or "They had a lot of rules that they imposed on me," or "They were really strict," or "They don't know what it's like in this generation." Figure out how to work with what you've got and where you are right now. How can you get the things you'd like to have in your life and not continue to be in conflict? Stop focusing on what you missed out on or blaming somebody else. Your parents are the way they are, but it's *your* life.

Effective Parenting

What if you are a parent yourself and want to raise empowered children? Know that helping somebody else achieve a sense of purpose is part of the mission of what it means to be a parent, but you can't do it for them. So if you've got some surly teenagers in your family, for example, the best thing you can do for them is to be a model of enlightened behavior. Remember, you get treated the way you teach people to treat you, so be an example of somebody who isn't going to allow someone else's behavior to disrupt even one hour of your life.

You can make it clear that you're there to help them, you can have talks with them, you can explain what you're doing, but ultimately they will know that you mean what you're all about by how you live, rather than by what you say or what you tell them to do. That's crucial. In other words, if your child comes home from school with a poor grade, is that a reason for you to ruin a day of your life? Ask yourself whose problem this is—why are you going to make it yours by becoming upset?

Now, I don't believe in ignoring somebody and letting them permissively do whatever they want. You can do things like restrict certain kinds of privileges. Or you can help them by enlisting tutors and the like. What you should never do is get yourself all worked up and become miserable in your life. You can be a caring parent while also teaching them that their behavior is just that, *theirs*. When they own it, they take responsibility for their actions and accept the consequences for it as well.

When I talk to parents who find themselves with disrespectful kids, I ask them what their behavior is like toward those children. They often respond that they make their lunches, do their laundry, and so on. Let's say you've got a child who calls you names, and your response is, "Oh, he's just finding himself . . . I'll make his lunch and then I'll chauffer him to his sports practice or pick him up from school." What incentive is there for this kid to change?

Another approach would be to tell him, "I can't force you to be respectful to me or put words in your mouth, but I certainly don't have to reward you for it. I'm going to show you that when you want to behave that way, then you're going to have to do that in isolation away from me. I'm not going to be somebody who's going to continuously wait on you and be your servant."

I believe that children learn by doing, not by somebody else doing things for them. If you have children over the age of eight and are still doing their laundry, for instance, you ought to be examining why that is. An eight-year-old is perfectly capable of working a washing machine and a dryer. It's a very simple little thing: you do their laundry for eight years, they do yours for eight years, and then you alternate for the remaining time they live with you. That seems to make a lot of sense.

Whenever you ask yourself what you owe your children, know the following: You don't owe them a slave. You don't owe them being a victim. You don't owe them sacrificing your life. What you do owe them is being the model of a loving, caring human being who is responding with ability to the circumstances of your own life, who has a sense of meaning and mission that is beyond your children. When your children see that in you, they will naturally come along. When you encourage independence, yes, that does mean they won't be dependent on you. Another benefit is that you are permitting them to try, to make mistakes, and to do all the things that go along with growing up to be a healthy person. Mostly, you don't model that you're going to tolerate bad behavior.

Imagine you're in a store with your child and they say they want a piece of bubblegum. You say they can't have it, but they don't let it go. You go round and round on this until they start to scream, and you give in. "All right," you say. "You want a piece of bubblegum, here's some money for the machine." Well, the message you've just sent is: *If you want a piece of bubblegum, you have to be crazy.* That's what you've taught your child.

Every child in the world has pulled this number with the bubblegum, including my own kids. Whenever that happened—that is, I'd say no and they'd start to cry—I'd say, "Hold it. That's terrific. Let's get everybody over here, we're going to put on a show." In other words, I showed them that such behavior would not be encouraged or tolerated. I was not going to be intimidated, bulldozed, manipulated, or victimized by them.

If your children are disrespectful toward you, yet you continue to make their lunches, do their housework, act as their chauffer, and give them money indiscriminately, all you're doing is saying, *I would like you to continue being nasty toward me. Here, let me reinforce it.* I don't think we should be doing that.

I also don't believe we should keep our children away from any sense of struggle. So many parents I know remember going out and hustling jobs, trying to cut grass and shovel snow and so on. A lot of us can remember earning our own nickels, dimes, and quarters—and we now have children who expect to drive sports cars or wear expensive clothes or have every little thing their heart desires, with parents who also pick up after them and take them everywhere.

I very much like this old saying: "Give a man a fish, and you feed him for a day. Teach a man to fish, and you feed him for a lifetime." There's a whole lot of truth in there when it comes to parenting. In order to have kids who are true successes, don't deny them the very thing that made you the successful person you are. Let them go out and work, and let them have some struggle. Allow them to enjoy learning their own lessons on their journey along the path of enlightenment.

Teaching Self-Worth

I've talked a bit about failure in this book already, but I'd like to revisit it here. Since the whole concept of failure is a judgment, it can actually be seen in a very positive light. I have failed many times, and I look at it as motivation. The most successful people are willing to fall down in life, a lot. And every time they do, they get up, dust themselves off, and say, "Well, that didn't work. I know not to do that now."

I'm always reminded of the story of Thomas Edison's endeavor to invent the lightbulb. After trying like 10,000 different times, he still hadn't come up with a commercially viable product. A reporter asked him, "Mr. Edison, how does it feel to have failed ten thousand times? For someone as famous as you, it must be awful."

He responded, "I don't even know what you're talking about, failure. Today I know ten thousand ways not to make a lightbulb. What do you know?"

Failure is only bad when you equate it with your self-worth, when you say, "Because I failed at something, that makes me a failure as a person." The healthiest place you can get to is the one where you're willing to try virtually anything. No-limit people are this way—they'll try anything, and they're not afraid. They don't live by the rules. They don't live by customs, traditions, or anyone else's dictates.

When I go in front of an audience, my self-worth is intact. It comes from myself, which is why it's called *self-worth*. If people like me, that's nice. If they applaud and laugh and enjoy, that's great—it's certainly better than if they don't. I like approval, but I don't need it. If I did need it, that would mean that when I didn't get it, I'd collapse. That's what a need is, isn't it? I'll tell you what I need—

I need oxygen, and I don't mind admitting it. But approval? That is an external motivation, not the goal of what I do.

I know people who have gone before an audience and focused on the one person who didn't clap or laugh, telling themselves, *See? I knew I wasn't any good. I have no value.* That's ridiculous. Focusing on one person who doesn't like what you say makes their opinion count more than your own self-worth. Remember, what others think of you is none of your business!

Self-worth comes from the belief that *I have integrity, I am valuable, I am attractive, I am important.* You don't have to go around saying it; instead, you have a quiet love affair with yourself. This is something you can teach your kids as well.

I wrote a book called *What Do You Really Want for Your Children?* because I think this is a very important question to ask. I know that I want the same things for my own children as I want for every child of our world. We're all in this thing together, so I'd like for them to grow up believing that they have a choice, and then to realize that empowerment.

When my daughter Tracy was in the second grade, she came home very upset. "Billy doesn't like me!" she cried.

"I understand, this is Billy's day," I told her. "This is one of the things Billy does on Tuesdays. Do *you* like you?"

"Yeah, of course I like me."

I said, "Well, that's all you've got."

She felt better right away; she was used to her daddy talking to her like this.

Some of the other parents in the neighborhood might have told their children, "Oh my goodness, what can we do to get Billy to like you? Let's see. Maybe we can invite him to a party. Maybe we'll let him play with your toys.

We'll do whatever we can." My feeling was that even a young child didn't have to learn that another's behavior toward her ought to be anything that brought her down. I still stand by this.

My children didn't grow up on fighting—and I have eight of them. They never had fighting reinforced as something that was normal; rather, they always had a belief system that it *wasn't* normal to fight and be angry and hate one another. Those impulses are things that we can learn to tame or not have at all, because fighting and anguish and pain and despair are things that bring us down and destroy our lives. My children have grown up with different attitudes about almost everything, but one of the things I am most proud of is that they are all full of love.

Expressing to the World What's Inside You

As I've taught my children, every second you spend upset, angry, hurt, or in despair because of the behavior of someone else, that is a moment in which you have given up control of your life. It's a moment in which you have said to the people in your world, "What you think of me is more important than what I think of myself, so I will do whatever I have to do to get you to like me."

Here's something to work on instead. Repeat the following to yourself: *I fill myself with love, and I send that out into the world. Those who accept it, that's wonderful; those who don't, that just happens to be where they are now. There is a karma to this planet that I'm only beginning to understand, but one thing I know is the importance of taking responsibility for my suffering, for my pain, for my difficulty. I understand that when I send out love as my reaction to anybody else's anguish, I will get love back.*

You can think of the universe as if it were a bank, and one of the nicest things about it is that it pays the highest interest rate there is. Let's say you sent out $1,000 worth of love; you'd receive about $1,300 every time. You'll get your $1,000 back to prove that what goes around comes around, and then you'll get a bonus. And the bonus is there to remind you that this loving way is the way to behave toward everyone.

Because the universe returns to you what you send out, it is imperative that you are a person of integrity. The highest place you can get to is one in which you are a person who follows through on whatever you say; that is, whatever comes out of your mouth is always consistent with the beliefs you have. You might exaggerate to make a joke, but you won't do so just to make yourself look better and impress others.

This need to distort reality, where does it come from? Why do we need to do that? No one cares. Understand that when you're lying in any way, it is a distortion; if you distort for long enough, it becomes a habit. You can always correct that habit, though. Whether you call it integrity or the ability to live by example for your children, it's so important to live what you say rather than to pretend to be something different than you are.

As I've mentioned, I am what I write about. That is, what I've written is what I am living each day of my life. It's important to work on getting yourself to that same integrity point, where what comes out of you is exactly what is in your heart. If you're going to try to make a difference with your children or in the world at large, then you do that by being a model of enlightenment. Any time you detract from that example, you are not being authentic, and being authentic is part of being enlightened.

You can't be cheating on your taxes while punishing your children for being dishonest and be an authentic, enlightened person at the same time. You can't be blowing cigarette smoke in their faces while telling them about the evils of addiction and be an authentic, enlightened person. You can't be out of shape and living a slobby lifestyle while telling your children about the importance of nutrition and be an authentic, enlightened person. You can't expect anybody that you work with in any business capacity to want to listen to what you say if what you say is different from what you are. It's crucial to understand how important being authentic is to everyone in your life and to all of humankind.

JOURNAL EXERCISE

Take some time to think about your childhood. Was it a happy one, or do you feel as if you missed out on some critical things? Do you need to work on a relationship with your parents from a space of forgiveness? Do you feel that you'd benefit from experiencing a happy childhood now? Write down in your journal some ways in which you could let your inner child out to bring more joy into your life now, regardless of what you've gone through in the past.

Next, if you are a parent, think about the relationship you have with your own children. Do you see yourself making mistakes with your kids that you'd like to remedy? Or are you encouraging their no-limit selves? (If you don't have children yourself, think about those in your family or friend group, or any kids around you who serve as inspirations for you.) Write down your impressions, as well as any other thoughts you have about being a parent or a child. How are you being a model of enlightenment for those in your life, and for all of humanity?

CHAPTER 8

LEAD

WITH

LOVE

Many large corporations have hired me over the years to come in and talk to them, which may seem surprising. At first glance, it would appear that what I have to offer them is a philosophy that's incompatible with business, but it isn't at all. Because when you take away all the people from General Motors or Chrysler or AT&T, you don't have a GM or a Chrysler or an AT&T—you have a lot of equipment that will rust away on you. All business is in the business of people. Every company is best served by human beings who are happy, fulfilled, and feeling good about themselves, not those who are having financial problems, loaded down with addiction, worried about their relationships falling apart, consumed by depression and anxiety. No matter how big the corporation, it behooves them to have a humanistic approach to running their business.

To that end, more and more companies are beginning to offer places where employees can go to exercise, keeping their bodies in good shape. But they are also offering spaces for workers to meditate or do yoga, thus endeavoring to keep their minds in good shape—at peace and in peak condition. It seems that employers are realizing the importance of helping workers condition their brains along with their bodies, and it's really wonderful to see. Again, the secret to all this is love.

The Big Picture

A lot of studies have been done on the difference in business between leaders and followers, and it seems that there are two things that really separate them:

1. Leaders always see the big picture, or the connection to the whole. If you've got a large corporation, the problem-oriented follower is somebody who sees only their job and what they have to do within their department. So they get trained to do this particular thing and don't really see how it impacts the next department and the entire company and its shareholders. They'll say things like, "It's not my department. I don't do those things. It's not my responsibility. You'll have to go to accounting to get that, or you'll have to call shipping." And they stay that way—it's like they have this quality for their entire lives, in which they have no connection to the whole.

The solution-oriented leader, on the other hand, sees that everything a person does in their job affects not only their department but also the next department and the entire company and the profit picture and so on. A leader is conscious of the entire business unit, and that person will almost always be elevated to positions of leadership because they're not just narrowly looking at *How does what I do affect me?*

2. Leaders anticipate the long-range effect of everything that is being done. For example, if they're on an airplane and see a flight attendant being rude to a customer, the leader recognizes how that behavior impacts the entire organization in the moment as well as how it will impact future business for years to come. They know that if a customer has a bad experience with a person on the airline, it isn't that individual who is going to feel the impact of such displeasure, because that employee is soon out of their life. The next time this customer needs to fly, though, they're going to pick a different airline altogether, and they might continue to take their business elsewhere for 10 years—and they will probably tell their friends, who will make the same decision. In other words, the long-range effects of one follower's rudeness to a customer can impact the entire airline dramatically.

Leaders understand such long-term effects. But they aren't just being polite and service-oriented and kind and decent to people because that's what they've been trained to do; they are being that way because that's the way they *are*. As a result, they truly see their connection to the organization as a whole and the bigger picture too.

And that's really what this is all about—the biggest picture of all. That is, how you behave toward your fellow humans affects you and them, and it also affects all of us. If you're thinking only about your particular organization and how someone's behavior impacts the organization now or in the future, then you're still limiting yourself. You have to look at the impact on your community, your country, and the world. I see the biggest picture of all, which ripples throughout all of humanity, and you can do the same.

You can apply the principles of leadership in your daily business and in your family and in your relationships, but you can expand them outward as well. You begin to take note of every negative or hostile act, every person who is not in harmony, because you know that when enough of us get into harmony, it impacts the entire planet.

We have to be able to extend our vision if we're thinking of ourselves as leaders. It's one thing to be a great leader within our corporation or department, or even within our own family, but another thing completely to be a great leader of humankind, and we all have to see ourselves that way.

"Coulda, Woulda, Shoulda"

Anybody who's a leader in any field is somebody who has trusted their inner signals, rather than somebody who's "played the game the right way." Inner-directedness is more than just being a rebel, though. It is like every operational phase of your life: You don't get up and do the things that you do because you're supposed to or because other people are telling you to. You're doing them because they make the greatest amount of sense to you. We all have those inner signals, or instincts, about what is right for us, but we seldom follow them. Too often we think about what we should do, what we must do, what we ought to do, instead of what is right for us.

Would, could, should, might, maybe, and *must* are the things that self-defeating folks are made of: *We could have done it this way. If only we would have done it this way. We should have done it that way.* Yet if you were a no-limit person, you'd understand that you've done everything in life the way you have because you were supposed to do it— otherwise you wouldn't have done it. The evidence that you were supposed to do it is that you did it. You can't not do it. You can't "should have done" anything. "If only" doesn't exist. You did it.

All my life I've heard people talk about what they "coulda, woulda, shoulda" done. The fact is that no one can ever "could have done" anything other than what they did. It's impossible.

Once I was in Minnesota in October to give a talk, and I said to my driver, "It's beautiful here. Look at the leaves, what fantastic colors."

He said, "Ah, this is nothing. You shoulda been here last week."

I replied, "But I could never 'shoulda been here last week' this week."

He looked at me like, *Oh boy. I got one of those crazy shrinks.*

Or here's something that happened to me several years ago, when I called the power company on a Friday. I said, "I'd like to have my electricity turned on."

The clerk replied, "You should have called on Wednesday."

"I beg your pardon. Hello? What are you talking about? Is this Earth?"

"Of course it's Earth."

I said, "Well, on Earth, where I've lived all my life, you can never 'should have called on Wednesday' on Friday. You can't do that."

"I think you better talk to my supervisor."

What a classic self-defeating response. It took me four supervisors before I got someone who understood that I didn't want to be told what I should have done on Wednesday, because on Friday you can never "could have called on Wednesday." You can't do that here. You can't go into rewind and go backward.

It's amazing how many people lead their lives that way, though. I like to tell my audiences this fun fact: Do you realize that if you would have bought five shares of Coca-Cola stock in 1916, you would be a millionaire today? Sure, most people I speak to weren't even born yet, but I can see them thinking, *I could have been.* Don't you hear people talking like that all the time?

When I play doubles tennis with my partner, I like to do something like this to amuse myself. I'll be covering the alley, and a shot will go right by me. He'll say, "You should have covered the alley."

I'll tell him, "I never could have 'should have covered the alley.' No one can do that."

He'll say, "Just cover the damn alley!"

That I can do. I can cover the alley, but I can't "should have covered" the alley. You see?

Telling people what they should have done is not constructive. How many times have your kids come home at five o'clock when they were supposed to have called you at three? When you tell them, "You should have called at three o'clock," the kid knows that's insane, because you can never "should have called at three o'clock." Now, if you say to him, "Tomorrow, if you don't call at three o'clock, the following things are going to happen . . . ," that's perfect. Then he has a complete understanding. But berating somebody for what they should have or could have or would have done is a waste of time.

Don't Send Your Ducks to Eagle School

There's an old saying in management, and this is something for you to commit to memory: *Don't send your ducks to eagle school.* Think about that. We've got a lot of ducks in the world and not many eagles, and trying to get a duck to become an eagle is one of the toughest jobs you'll run into in life. There are problem-oriented ducks everywhere, and precious few eagles who are willing to soar beyond limits.

See, ducks think in duck-like ways, and when you try to train them to be eagles, they don't seem to get the message. They tend to be stuck on "impossibility," the notion that *Well, we've always done things this way. This is just the way we do it. It's impossible to change.*

I remember thinking about this once on an airplane as I watched the flight attendants serve drinks in a completely inefficient way. The meals had been served, and then way up at the front was this cart, which meant that the way they were going, most of us weren't going to get our drinks until the meal was done. I like to have something to drink while I'm eating, as most people do, and I wondered, *Why do they only take one order at a time?* There were three people on each side of the aisle, and the flight attendant would ask each person what they wanted. She would then get a cup and put in the ice, and then she'd pour in the drink and hand it to the customer. She did this every time, for six people, and then went to the next row.

Now, an eagle would have asked, "All right, what do you six people want?" and been ready to go. For some reason, the ducks didn't believe in this approach. They seemed to feel, *Hey, if you get there, you get there. If it happens, it happens. If you get something to drink an hour after the flight is over and you're getting your bag, so be it.* It's very similar to the attitude of our old friend in the grocery store, the one-bagger.

Ducks are everywhere, I tell you. I was in line at a bank not too long ago, and the teller seemed to be on terminal hold with someone on the phone. I was the next person in line, and she had been in this position for so long that I finally asked her, "Could you please help me? I just want to deposit this check and get out of here."

"Sir, I can only do one thing at a time!" she quacked.

I said, "Only one? I could do ten things at a time."

After all, if you want to be an eagle, you've got to be looking out for the mice down here, you've got to be looking out for telephone poles, you've got to be thinking about your little eaglets. You've got a million things to do at once! Who among us can only do one thing at a time? Certainly, no parent could ever fall into this category. With little ones, you have to learn how to read a book while you're watching them swim, and help them with their homework while you're making dinner. You just learn how to do all this when you're an effective person. You for sure don't sit around and say, "I can only do one thing at a time, kids."

I remember being in one great big duck pond when I was a child myself. We had a teacher tell us, "This is the worst class I've ever had! I cannot stand it!" Many in the class felt guilty on hearing this, but my response was to think, *This is the worst class she's ever had? Her life must be great. We're so easy! Why is she setting up this guilt pattern?* Sure enough, many of the other kids went home and felt bad and manipulated, but not me.

I've since run into this kind of mentality everywhere. I once stayed at this lovely hotel in Orlando, Florida, and they put me on the ninth floor, which was called the concierge level. They charged $100 more a night for these rooms, but they came with concierges to take care of you.

The first night I was there, they had hot appetizers from 7 P.M. to 9 P.M. I had gone running and didn't get back until about 9:10, but I asked if I could take some appetizers back to my room.

The concierge said, "No problem. The kitchen's closed, but I'm happy to go down there and bring some up to you. They've also got a nice little dessert— would you like some of that as well?"

"That would be great."

This guy had no idea who I was or anything like that, but he went out of his way for me and that was terrific!

The next morning, however, they had a continental breakfast that ended at 9:30 A.M. Again, I was out during that time, but I returned a few minutes afterward and asked for some juice. This time, I ran into a duck, who quacked, "Sir, continental breakfast closes at 9:30. I'm sorry."

I said, "I know that. I understand, but all I'd like is some orange juice. I'm really thirsty. I just finished running, and I have to give a talk in a little while."

She said, "Sir, 9:30. It says so very clearly."

I'm the guy paying $100 more a night for the concierge, and she's dismissing me. You see the difference? The difference is an attitude. It's one person's belief.

Now, I can assure you that if you follow these two concierges, you're going to see something much like the one-bagger versus the two-bagger. You're going to see that eagle soaring all through his life, and the duck is going to go from that job to probably one a little more demeaning, always wondering why.

If I were looking for somebody to work for me, I would simply go observe bag boys for a day, and I'd know whom to hire. In my experience, great employees are not trained; they're found. You go out there and find those people who have that two-bagger, eagle-like attitude, then you can help them to do and be anything.

This makes me think of something I once experienced at O'Hare Airport in Chicago. I was set to get on a flight in the afternoon to fly down to Fort Lauderdale, when they canceled my flight.

I said to the fellow, "That's okay, because I know you have a flight 45 minutes from now that goes to West Palm Beach. That's only 20 miles away. You can go ahead and put me on that flight, and I'll get to Fort Lauderdale from there."

He looked in the computer and said, "I'm sorry, we can't do that."

"Why not—are there no seats?"

"No, sir, there are some empty seats, but the computer says that those are two separate cities."

"Miami and Fort Lauderdale are considered the same city," I retorted, "but Fort Lauderdale and West Palm are considered different cities?"

He said it would be the same as if I had asked to go to San Francisco. "It's a different city as far as the computer is concerned. We can't do that. I'm sorry, but you'll have to take a flight four hours from now. We've got you covered, and you'll be on that flight."

"You mean you canceled my flight but won't let me on one that's 20 miles from the airport that I want to go to because the computer says it's a separate city?"

He said, "That's right. I'm sorry, there's nothing else I can do." Of course, this is a phrase we've all heard countless times.

I said, as I usually do, "I'd like to talk to somebody else—anybody else, please."

"I'm sorry, sir, if I bring out a supervisor, he's going tell you the same thing." And he started to leave.

I said, "Wait, don't go." I knew he was about to return to the duck pond. "Go upstairs. Just go up some stairs, any stairs, and see if you can find an eagle."

"What on earth are you talking about?"

I explained, "I don't care who it is, but please bring out somebody who doesn't already believe it can't be done. That's the only kind of person I want. I don't want a guarantee or anything like that. I want to talk to a human being who doesn't believe 'it can't be done.'" Sure enough, he did just that. He found me an eagle, who was able to get me on the flight I wanted. Everything worked out the way it was supposed to.

You must understand that the world is full of ducks, and you have to really watch out that you don't become one yourself. Remember, success is an inner process. When you have it inside of you, you consequently bring success to everything you do, and you can soar through life.

JOURNAL EXERCISE

Think about the times when you've encountered ducks or eagles in your life—do either of these types remind you of yourself? In your journal, write down your feelings about this. How might you become more of a leader yourself, by shining the light of your love to show others the way?

PART III

THE MISSION OF YOUR LIFE

*Have the courage to follow your passion
—and if you don't know what it is,
realize that one reason for your
existence on earth is to find it.*

— OPRAH WINFREY

CHAPTER 9

A
SENSE
OF
PURPOSE

In the last few years I worked in schools, I tried to put together a curriculum to train young people on how to be the healthiest human beings they could be. If you're a parent and someone were to ask you what you want for your children, you'd probably answer with something like, "I want them to be happy, I want them to be fulfilled, I want them to have a sense of purpose in their lives." But where can they go to learn this? Where are the courses on how to avoid feeling guilty, how not to think anxiously, how not to worry about what other people think of you, how to eliminate approval seeking all the time, how to love yourself, how to live in the present rather than in the future or the past, how not to allow yourself to be victimized, and how to manage your own emotions? How come kids don't take classes on those subjects?

As we've discussed in this book, one of the crucial variables of the no-limit person is that they are internally motivated. They consult their inner signals to decide what is right or wrong for them, and to determine their own life mission and how they're going to follow it. Most children instinctively listen to their intuition, but then they get into schools and are essentially taught to ignore it. If you go into any given school and ask for their philosophy of education, you'll be told something like, "We at this particular school encourage the full self-development and individual self-actualization of each child we attempt to educate. We want to provide curricular interventions that will give individual development and specific self-actualization goals to each child that comes through our door."

And that is so much nonsense. Because in fact when you see young people beginning to display the qualities of being awakened and transformed, of saying to the teachers and the principals and the administrators, "Wait a second. Why? How come we have these kinds of regulations? Couldn't we change some of these things?" they are shut down. You have kids saying, "I'd like to study this, and that seems to make more sense to me," challenging authority and so on, but we don't listen to them. I'd like to see us stop doing just about everything we can in our schools to douse the sparks of internal motivation.

After all, everybody I've ever met wants to feel special, unique, and significant. Without exaggeration, I believe nothing can be more important to us than to have a daily sense of purpose, or mission, about our life. We all want to leave indelible footprints on the world, yet we seem to have our priorities for doing so all out of whack.

Transcend the Rules

One of my favorite quotes of all time comes from Henry David Thoreau: "If one advances confidently in the direction of his dreams, and endeavors to live the life which he has imagined, he will meet with a success unexpected in common hours."

I alluded to this a bit in the last part of the book, but to me this means that when you take chances and work confidently toward doing the things that mean something to you—that is, you're not focused on following the rules, being a good employee or spouse or parent, or the like—living your life *your* way, then success follows you in ways you never dreamed were possible before. But if you're chasing anything outside yourself, like bigger paychecks or more lavish vacations, you might be doing what you're "supposed" to do, but you won't have inner peace. And when you lack inner peace, you lack a reason for living. You lack a sense of purpose. You're just sort of coping, telling yourself, *For God's sake, get out there, don't make any trouble, don't make any waves, and get along with the world.* This is certainly no way to live the life of your dreams.

From the time we are very young, we're conditioned to act in accordance with a set of rules and guidelines, and we go on to follow them for the majority of our lives. These rules include:

- *Do whatever you're supposed to do, and nothing you're not supposed to do.*
- *Do what you're told, and don't ask questions.*
- *Go to school and get good grades. Don't give your teachers a hard time.*
- *Get into college if you can. If you can't, go out and get a job.*

- *Get the training you need to bring home a decent paycheck.*
- *Get married; have children; raise a family.*
- *Please other people, as much as you possibly can.*
- *Pay your bills on time.*
- *Don't go to jail; in fact, stay out of trouble altogether.*
- *Make as much money as you can.*
- *Dress well and have nice toys.*
- *Go to parties and have a few drinks.*
- *Do all the things that will make your life work. Go along to get along.*

Then something happens to change your priorities. Maybe you have a health scare, or you simply realize that you don't have all the time in the world. Whatever the reason, this is when you tend to find your mission as a human being. You can do all those things that I listed above— follow the rules and be good and please other people—and you will get through your life with a minimum of trouble, staying out of jail and so on. However, it is impossible to have a sense of purpose in your life by following those rules. It's just not possible.

For example, the rules instruct you to *Save for the future, think about when you retire, focus on your objectives,* and that's fine. You'll certainly need to do this if you've got kids going to college or things of that nature, but it won't give you a sense of purpose or meaning to your life. If you try to find a purpose by living life through your children, you'll always be frustrated, even though you'll be a wonderful parent. By definition, you cannot feel fulfilled by someone else's accomplishments; you can only stand back and vicariously watch them. That is, you can't get the sense of what *you* are doing here on this planet.

A sense of purpose comes from learning the exact opposite of what the rules preach—and part of my mission is to change your thinking on this subject. I want you to see that your priority in life must be whatever your passion or calling is. Transcending the rules happens when you move away from "more, more, more," or "better, better, better." Instead of being externally motivated and taking your cues from the things outside yourself, you're consulting your inner signals, what you believe to be right for you.

When you follow the rules, you get up in the morning and go to that job you no longer feel fulfilled by—you've mastered it, you know how to do it, the challenge of it is no longer there. Understand that if you go through your life doing what you've always done, and there's no challenge or creativity left in it, it has become routine or "drill." Think about soldiers marching in formation—well, that's what your life has become. Drill is not fulfilling. It just keeps you automatically responding to what you've been doing for the external paycheck, and the inner peace you want isn't there. When you're following your purpose, however, you leave any sense of drill behind.

You may be thinking about your responsibilities and all the risks it would take to focus on your personal mission. We'll talk about this in more detail later on, but it turns out that most people who take risks do better than they ever did before: They end up making more money, even though they're not looking for it. They end up with improved health and better relationships, as well as more time for the truly important things in life, such as spending time with their loved ones and the like.

I see so many people out there who spend their lives struggling to keep up with the Joneses, solely focused on external motivation. And I think to myself, *If you could only understand that there's so much more to life than this.*

Our focus must shift to advancing confidently in the direction of our dreams.

Life Is a Masterpiece

The fact is that most of us in Western culture define who we are and how well we're doing on the basis of some very artificial criteria, such as *How much money am I making? How much stuff is coming into my life? How many accolades am I able to collect?* This is not the yardstick to use for measuring our humanity, for determining whether or not we're living the kind of life we're capable of.

Another thing we tend to laud in our culture and almost worship is performance. You see it all the time, people making a contest out of life, with performance being measured in terms of *How far have I gotten? What position have I achieved? What awards have been granted to show that I'm number one?* The other is achievement: *How far have I gone in my profession? How am I looked at by my peers and by other people with respect to my grades or my position at a given corporation?*

We're always talking about accomplishment, achievement, and performance; they're almost like the ultimate objectives in our culture. What has happened for me and many others is that after we lived this type of life for a while—accomplishing a lot of things, performing at a very high level, and achieving so many external rewards—we soon discovered there was an emptiness to all of it. We had the feeling that we were simply in pursuit of gratifying our egos and proving we could accumulate as much stuff as possible.

When success is no longer measured by how you're serving others but how much you're getting for yourself, it can turn into obsession. Many people have fallen into this trap of believing that they have to continually accumulate more and perform at a higher level. If they win the championship, that's great, but how about doing it two times in a row? Nobody's ever done that before. If they do it twice in a row, now they've got to do it three times in a row, and now they also have to do it by shutting out their opponents completely. Nothing is ever enough.

When you get caught in this trap of constantly looking outside yourself for those artificial ways of defining yourself as a human being, you find there's a lack of passion or fulfillment. What would it be like to instead live your life as a work of art, a masterpiece that is unfolding in every moment?

This is what I have begun to do. Instead of looking at my life in terms of how much I can get or how far I can go, I am now seeing it as this fabulous work of art. I can shape and shade and mold it into whatever I think would be the absolute ideal for my contribution while I'm here on this planet, for the actual unfolding of my humanity, my purpose.

When I think of an ideal example of someone who lived their life like a masterpiece, I don't think of how much stuff this person had or how big their bank account was or how fast they ran or whom they beat in the process. Rather, the answer is found on a much higher level for me. I look to the lives of people like Jesus Christ, Mohammed, and Buddha; that is, spiritual masters who gave us a potent message about the power of the human mind. More recent times have brought us examples in the form of Mahatma Gandhi, who was able to turn around the whole fate of a nation that had been subservient to the British Empire. He was able to do it all through nonviolence and an approach to loving people, not conflict or something that had to be debilitating or destructive. He put the people of India on a course of running their own lives, all through a sense of beauty and appreciation. This is so inspiring to me.

Please understand that I'm not here to put down, in any sense of the word, performance and achievement. I'm a person who has a lot of those things in my life, but as the years pass, I've found that they mean less and less to me. Yet they've shown up more as I've become more tuned in to something higher. It's like a knowingness of what I'm here for, how I'm going to live this life I have in the service of others.

It's vital to maintain a sense of spirituality about yourself, a sense of compassion and caring and love and decency for everyone you meet. Treat conflict and difficulties that come your way as opportunities to learn how to transcend them. You don't have to use hatred and anger and bitterness and beating somebody else down in order to get to this higher place of purpose.

Finding your calling doesn't mean abdicating your role in life; it doesn't mean you can no longer do whatever it is you choose to do for a living. You're just coming from a place of peace now. When you begin to see that you can make your life unfold exactly the way the universe unfolds, with a real sense of perfection and harmony and peace for yourself, your life indeed becomes a wonderful work of art.

The more you do this, the paradox is that all the things you chased after so hard and so diligently will show up in your life in the right amounts. You'll have surrendered—not to another person, but away from the things that most people are pursuing all their lives. They're stuck on that stress-filled, fast-paced treadmill that insists, *I have to achieve. I have to perform. I have to become number one. I have to beat everybody else in order to prove myself.* But you will have developed an inner sense of harmony and know that those kinds of things are very low-level determiners of what kind of a human being you are. You are focused on something much more important now: the mission of your life.

Focus on the Present Moment

You can't live a life of purpose in the future or the past. You must do it now, today, in this moment. In fact, one of the concepts that you really need to get into your head, which will free you from thinking in a ego-driven way, is the concept of *now*. We in the West are not very good at now. It can seem as if we don't even know what it means, because we fill ourselves with a lot of worries about our responsibilities and following the rules. We concentrate on being good family people, going to work every day, paying the bills, and doing all the things we're supposed to do. Again, all those things are fine, but they will not fill any of us with any kind of passion.

When you live in the now, you allow yourself the freedom to enjoy a moment, rather than postponing that gratification or joy because you've got something more pressing to do. As mentioned, money, prestige, promotions, awards, and other achievements can never truly give you a sense of purpose. They might pay your mortgage or provide you with something to put on a shelf or hang on your wall, but they are all external motivations.

What *does* give you a sense of purpose are your internal motivations; that is, what you feel about yourself, how you evaluate what you are, and how much you're growing and experiencing the world. When you're focused on these things, you're no longer looking for your life's mission—it will find you. Like happiness and success, purpose is something you *are,* and you will bring it to everything that you have and do in your life.

Now, I think goals and plans are important for all of us to have. We simply have to keep in mind that every step on the way to the achievement of the goal is equally as important as every other step, and you don't want to fall so deeply in love with a plan that there is no room for adjustment. Let's say that before you set out on a trip, you planned out every stop ahead of time, making reservations all along the way. Then when you're on the road, you get to a place you've never been before that's very intriguing. Maybe they're having a rodeo the next day, and you'd really like to stay and see that—but you can't, because your plan, your goals, your objectives are ruling you rather than you ruling your life. If you can't adjust and be flexible with the things you want for yourself, then that is unhealthy.

Making plans and setting goals can be quite healthy as long as it's kept in the spirit of now, of staying in the present moment. I'll give you an example from my own life. One October many years ago, I ran my very first marathon. When I started running a year or so before that, I didn't have any idea about participating in a marathon. I just wanted to see if I could run each day, one day at a time, whatever my body said I could do and at whatever pace I wanted to—that was the goal for me. I started one day, and the next day I decided to do it again, even though my shins were hurting and I was out of breath. And then I did it on the next day, and the next day, and so on.

After three or four weeks, instead of running one and a half miles, I was running two miles. I hadn't upgraded my goal; rather, my body allowed itself to go faster and farther, which is only natural. I continued on in that process of individual, daily goals for myself, which involved living in the present and enjoying myself. I then had an automatic kind of upgrading of those goals for myself—within a year, there I was at the starting line of a race to run 26.2 miles. Now, if you'd have said a year prior to this that I could do that, I would have thought, *You must be crazy to think anybody would even want to run 26 miles.*

By the way, I finished that marathon in three and a half hours. I couldn't believe it when I heard that some people had stopped running in a little over two hours. I told myself, *If you get out there and run for three and a half hours, then you've got something. If you stop after two hours, hell, anybody can do that.* I figured I won, since I ran longer than anybody in that race. As you know, it all comes back to attitude. It's what you believe.

Let's say you want to lose weight, quit smoking, or eliminate some other addictive behavior in your life. It seems to me that the only sensible way to attack a problem like losing weight is to say to yourself, *Today, just today, I will not eat sugar.* Or if you're quitting smoking, say, *Just today, I will go 24 hours without a cigarette.* Or whatever it may be. If someone asks me, "Can I really do that?" I'll answer, "Of course. Anybody can go a day. That's no big deal."

So you go through this one day. Then when you're at the end of that 24-hour period, you are a new person. Don't tell yourself, in a very ego-driven way, *I'm only going to want sugar tomorrow anyway. Who am I kidding? I'm going to want to have a hot fudge sundae tomorrow night, so I might as well have one tonight too.* Or, *You mean I can never have another sundae the rest of my life?* That'll drive you right to the refrigerator faster than anything. Don't do that to yourself, or you'll be eating hot fudge sundaes every night.

Instead, at the end of the day, say to yourself, *I now have a 24-hour history of no ice cream in my body. Or if you're trying to stop smoking, say, I now have a 24-hour history of no nicotine in my body.* After that one day, you're a different person, and you can let that person decide whether they want to go another day. Don't let the person who wants a cigarette or hot fudge sundae right now decide; let the person who has 24 hours of success behind them make the decisions. Then, the next day, you'll have 48 hours behind you, and on it goes.

You have the power to become a new person every day. Don't believe me? Ask anybody who's ever been in Alcoholics Anonymous, which firmly believes in the slogan *One day at a time.* You can handle anything this way, dealing with your life one day at a time. You can have a lot of goals in this day and not be living in the future at all. It would be absurd to say you should never have goals for yourself; everybody has a goal. It's how much you can do about it in the present moment that counts.

You have to live every day fully, rather than postponing your gratification or purpose in the pursuit of something in the future that may or may not arrive for you. And if it does, you will very likely be a completely different person anyway. That's one of the hardest things to understand. That is, if you set a goal for yourself for a distant point in the future, when you get there you're going to be a very different person from who you are now.

We only get present moments in which to live. Wanting to be something five years from now assumes that you're going to be here then, in this body, in the way you are living now. And that's quite an assumption. In other words, if you always have that five-year notion, there is going to come a time when you won't be able to achieve that. Because the future is promised to no one, and the past is gone like the wake of a boat. All we have to live in is the present moment.

Enjoy the Journey

One of the things that's important to learn how to do is to act as if what you want is already there. You don't act as if, *Maybe if I set all these goals and work really hard at them, then I'll get what I want. Boy, will I be excited once I finally get there.* Just as happiness and success are both inner concepts, so is fulfillment. If you think that you're going to find fulfillment by obtaining a goal you have worked really hard for, then your life is all about external striving. What you need is a psychology of arriving, not striving.

Think about this quote by Ralph Waldo Emerson: "To finish the moment, to find the journey's end in every step of the road, to live the greatest number of good hours, is wisdom." Or I'm sure you're familiar with the saying, "It's the journey, not the destination." I want you to see that every step along the way to realizing your goals is just as important to savor as getting there.

If you're focused only on striving, you cannot be a no-limit person. If you concentrate your energy solely on goals to reach in the future, you will always be a ego-dominated person who suffers from the "disease of more." When you reach your goal, you won't know what to do with it. You won't know how to handle what you've got now, so you'll upgrade your goal. If your goal is to get $100,000 and you get it, you'll then feel that you need to get $200,000, and so on. Your life will become about more struggling, more suffering, more trying to get there. And if you do ever "get there," all of a sudden you'll look around and realize you're an old person, and you'll wonder, *What happened to my life?*

There's absolutely nothing wrong with pursuing a goal as long as you stay consistent with the truth. The truth is the most important thing you can have in your life. As I previously mentioned, it's so important to have integrity, to get to the point where every word that comes out of your mouth is exactly as it is, and exactly as you are. If you slip up, that doesn't mean you're less than valuable. It simply means that you have something to learn from slipping. You learn to appreciate what you have to learn from slipping rather than saying, "I failed and that makes me bad. I guess I don't have integrity after all."

You see, the more you operate from goal setting in the sense of repairing deficiencies, the more your life becomes one of striving, and when you do arrive where you want to be, you won't know how to deal with that because your whole life has been in anticipation of it. There are a lot of people out there who, while having their first cup of coffee, are thinking about the second cup. While having an appetizer, they're wondering if they're going to be able to get a dessert. They're so focused on what's coming in the future that they don't take the time to savor what they have in the present.

One of the most enlightening and empowering things we can do is be able to make a peak experience out of a present moment—any present moment.

Think about what happened to the writer Fyodor Dostoyevsky, who lived in the 1860s in Russia under the czar. When Dostoyevsky was a young man, he was accused of being in alliance with a literary group in Moscow that was attempting to overthrow the czar by talking about subversive ideas like freedom, that people have a right to think for themselves and make choices.

So the czar accused Dostoyevsky of being a member of this group, and he was sentenced to die. He was put into a cell in Moscow and told the date of his execution. When the time came, Dostoyevsky was taken along with five other men to stand before a firing squad. They took a black shroud and wrapped it around the eyes of the first man, and then the czar's guards shot and killed him. They did the same to the next man in line, and Dostoyevsky got to watch all this happen right in front of him.

Then they put the shroud around his eyes and prepared to shoot him, as he was the next man in line to die. Dostoyevsky, the writer of some of the greatest books ever written! At the last moment, he and the other two men in the group were spared from death. For some reason the czar instead decided to punish them with 10 years of hard labor in prison.

Dostoyevsky went on to write about the value of the present moment and learning how to get consumed by it. For example, when he saw a cockroach in the cell where he had been condemned to die, it wasn't an annoyance. It wasn't some creature that was filthy that he didn't want to crush with his shoe. It was a miracle.

There's an old saying that life is what happens to you while you're busy making other plans. This is so true. You must understand that no matter where you are, every moment in your life is a miracle to be lived. Stop looking for miracles in something in the future, and enjoy every step along the path of enlightenment.

JOURNAL EXERCISE

Take a look at the list of rules I included earlier in the chapter. Do they resonate with you? That is, have you been living your life so far in accordance with these external motivators? Then think about what you might do instead, and write about that in your journal. Know that there is a very good chance that whatever you've just written about is pointing you in the direction of your purpose.

CHAPTER 10

FOLLOW

YOUR BLISS

I think we all show up here with a mission. We have lessons, things we have to learn as we travel the path of enlightenment. For some of us, it will take a short time; for others, it can take a very long time. Some people will have 30 years of experience, while others will have 1 year of experience 30 times. That is, some are focused on growth and getting as much out of life as possible, while others keep repeating the same thing over and over again. It's the two different approaches of the yaysayer and the naysayer, and not the same for everybody.

A good friend who's a doctor confessed to me, "You know, this practice is really wearing on me. I feel so burned out. Sure, I'm making a lot of money and all that, but I don't want to do this. I want to be a sportscaster." He thought he could practice on high school teams and fantasized about giving it a try.

I replied, "So why aren't you pursuing that? You're a physician and certainly that is a noble profession, but why would you want to continue in it if it's something you don't want to do?"

"I decided a long time ago what I was going to be, and I can't change that now. I'm a doctor—that's who I am."

"Who decided that you were going to be a doctor?" I asked him.

"I did. I made that decision when I was 18 years old."

I said, "Would you consult a teenager today to get vocational guidance for where you should be going in your life? Would you trust an 18-year-old for advice on that?"

"Why, of course not."

"But isn't that exactly what you're doing now?"

What happens if, like my friend, you want to alter plans that you set into motion years ago? If you got yourself into a career but have since come to find out you don't like it or it's no longer a challenge, you may feel that you can't change things because you're so locked into this plan. Well, if you're not happy or being fulfilled by what you're doing in this moment, you have the option to change it. You don't have to be attached to what you've been. What you've been is just the choices that you made once upon a time, and you always have the power to change your mind.

Let's say that when my friend was 18 and decided to be a physician, he then changed his mind once he got into medical school. That would have been okay! It wouldn't necessarily have been a horrendous kind of letdown or disappointment; in fact, making that change in plans probably would have brought him to where he really wanted to be in life much sooner.

Remember, what is considered failure can actually be an opportunity. So rather than continuing with a plan you know isn't right for you, simply say, "I think I'll move in this direction now," and find out what *is* right. Why would you want to spend one more second doing something you don't want to do? After all, no one knows how long their life will be. However, I can guarantee you that it will be a lot longer and more meaningful if you reframe your thinking and adapt the techniques I've talked about throughout this book.

Own Your Uniqueness

I can hear a collective rumbling in the world as I broach the subject of changing course in life. I'm sure many of you are thinking, *Yes, but I have responsibilities. Yes, but I have a mortgage. Yes, but . . .* There are a lot of those *Yes, but*s, and they spring from fear.

I want to make it very clear that you can't succeed unless you're willing to fail. Did you know that the same year Babe Ruth hit 60 home runs, he also had 89 strikeouts? If you want to hit home runs, you have to be willing to strike out. In the process, you'll have the chance to see where you are and how you're doing on your path.

This doesn't mean that you need to focus on being better than everybody else—because if you have to be a winner by defeating everybody else, then you'll always be a loser, because no one can always defeat everybody else, no matter how great they are. That's not a good definition of winning at all. If you're having to look over your shoulder at somebody else to decide how you're doing, then somebody else's performance is determining how well you're doing. No-limit people don't look at other people to gauge where they are. They say, "That's how that person is running. That's where they are in their music development, or whatever it is. It has nothing to do with me. Where I am is how I decide to be."

There is nothing wrong with getting out there and competing in a race or a golf match or what have you. But understand that its aim is not to evaluate who you are and how valuable you are, but rather to determine where your skills are in comparison to those you're competing against. And when the competition is over, it's over. It's also important to get to the point where you welcome failure, because that's how you learn. You don't learn much from a victory except to stay the same. But when you suffer a loss or fail at something, it's a wonderful experience because it gives you an opportunity to grow. So to me, this whole business of failing is not a concern at all.

Another fear is: *I won't be liked,* or *Somebody won't approve of me.* Awakened people do not run their lives by, or even pay attention to, what others think or say or tell them to do. Instead, they say, "I focus on what my own inner signals tell me to do. As long as I'm not hurting anybody else or interfering with their right to run their life as they choose, then anything I do is okay." That's all morality is, by the way: your right to swing your fist and flail around stops with my right to have my nose shaped the way I want it to be shaped. That's it. That's the only morality there is.

If you're trying to run your life based on external motivations such as what everybody else is saying or thinking or feeling, know that there's always going to be somebody—or a large number of somebodies—who are going to dislike it. You cannot please everyone all the time. It's impossible. Also, every great idea comes from an innovator, and innovators are people who do things differently and are not trying to please everybody else. When you think about it, if you try to please everyone else, or if you try to be just like everyone else, what do you personally have to offer? You'll have only sameness to offer.

It's time to own your uniqueness. It's important to recognize that no one will ever truly understand you, because you're special. You are a unique creation, and no one can ever get behind your eyeballs and see things as you do. Therefore, there's really only one boss in your life, and that's you. I know what the world of work is like out there—I've been in it all my life. I also know that the person looking back in the mirror at you is the one you truly have to answer to every day.

Take the Risk

If you're in a job in which you're feeling a measure of dissatisfaction, then the first thing you must do is change your attitude toward what you're currently doing. If a no-limit person got sentenced to solitary confinement, they'd know how to make that work for themselves. That's what anybody who was ever put under horrible conditions, like the survivors of Nazi concentration camps, was able to do. Whether it was a blade of grass, a ray of sunlight, a small bit of bread, the sharing of a beautiful story, whatever it was—they could take in the moment and live it fully. If people could do that under those conditions, I can't think of any job in the world in which you can't change your attitude toward it and make it better for you. Once you do that, by the way, your chances of being promoted or getting out of there and doing other things become greater.

If you've tried to change your attitude but still don't feel that sense of purpose that is so important, then it's time to take a risk. Change your circumstances; leave your job. You're not going to let your life fall apart. I assure you that if you have always paid your bills, then that is who you are. And that's the person you ought to consult, rather than the one who insists that a disaster is on the way if you make a choice to be something different. I like this quote attributed to Mark Twain: "I'm an old man and I've had many troubles. Most of which have never happened." Much of what you're envisioning that's so terrible, all the disasters you think are going to befall you as a result of taking that chance, is only in your head.

Get out there and do what you need to do—try the new job, get out of that relationship, move on to another part of the country or the world, do something you've always wanted to do. You may struggle at first, or you may not make as much money. Chances are, though, you'll actually do better. Most people find out that having a sense of personal mission about themselves is invaluable. There is no price tag you can put on how you feel each day when you're doing something that is important to you.

I am a classic example of what I'm talking about here. I was once a college professor and a therapist in New York, and I was doing a lot of workshops and things like that. I had a secure position at a major university, yet the idea of working for somebody else every day of my life just didn't give me the sense of purpose I wanted. So I said, "I don't want this. I'm going to write, I'm going to talk to people, and I'm going to go on television. I'm going to make this thing happen." Anyone who knew me before I became famous knows that this was something I announced to everyone, to all my classes and so on.

I heard from so many people that, "What the world needs least of all right now is another self-help book, and we certainly don't need another psychologist telling us what to do." But I couldn't have cared less. I wrote *Your Erroneous Zones* and found a publisher willing to take a chance on it. When they told me I couldn't get on network television to promote the book because I was an unknown, I said, "Fine, then I'll go on WBAB," which was a little five-watt station in Babylon, New York. That's where I did my very first interview. As I wrote earlier in this book, I went to other places where I could get on a radio or TV show and talk to whoever would listen.

When I was told my publisher wouldn't be providing copies of my book to sell in the towns I visited, I said, "That's no problem, I'll take them with me." When I heard they probably weren't going to do a second printing, I said, "Send me what's left of the first printing," and 2,000 books were delivered right to my garage one day. When the official word came that they definitely weren't going to do a second printing, I said, "Well, you don't have any of the first printing left; it's all sold out." Sure, I was the one who'd bought them, but they were still sold out.

I didn't have a whole lot of money and had to borrow some to buy those books, but I would do anything to make my dream happen. It was a matter of never once wavering from it. I'd go on a radio show and people would ask, "Where can we get your book?" I had a list of all the nearest bookstores in whatever town I was in, so I'd say, "You can get them at this bookstore over here and that bookstore over there." Pretty soon, the bookstores were getting phone calls for a book they didn't carry. Then I would arrive at the store with my little truck and copies of *Your Erroneous Zones*. I'd hear, "We've had several requests for that book already. Where is it?" I'd get them the copies and ask, "Do you want me to leave you a couple of cases? If you don't sell them, you can send them back to me." And they'd say sure. I became my own distributor, and the book finally sold out.

I went all across the country, doing countless interviews, driving between cities, going out there and spending money I didn't have. After I had made numerous attempts to appear on *The Tonight Show,* they finally called and said they'd like to have me come on, and the book took off from there.

After all this, do you know what I heard, over and over? "Boy, were you lucky, you hit it at the right time. Things really worked out for you." No one seemed to understand the amount of work that had gone into this "overnight success."

When I left the opportunity to have tenure for the rest of my life and a lot of external security and went across the country to talk about erroneous zones back in 1976, everyone told me how insane I was. But I've never listened to what everyone else said; I've always listened to who I am. I knew that no matter what, my inner signals were indicating that this was what I had to do. I could not be stopped from doing what I knew was right for me.

As I've said many times, writing has always just been something I am. It isn't anything I could ever quit. Regardless of whether I ever sold a single book, I love it. I feel so fulfilled when I write, knowing I'm leaving indelible footprints behind.

The irony is that after I finally resigned from being a professor and did what I really believed in and loved, I made more money in that first year than I had made the entire 35 years previously. That's right, in one year I made more money than I had in my entire life. And it wasn't because I was lucky or had any special breaks. I didn't have any more opportunity than anybody else. In fact, I had less. I came from complete poverty and many years in foster homes and orphanages, and I had to earn my own way through everything. No, it was because I was advancing confidently in the direction of my dreams. I went out there and lived the life I had imagined.

Love What You Do, and Do What You Love

Recently, I was talking to somebody who's worked at a factory in Indiana for 29 years. He explained that his real love is his apple orchard and its 300 trees. He knew so much about the different kinds of apples—how much water you have to give them, where you plant them, when you harvest them, and which pesticides are safe and which ones aren't. He's so excited about his apples, yet he spends 99 percent of his life doing something that he doesn't like.

I said, "Your bliss is your orchard, isn't it?"

His face broke out into a huge smile. "Ah, I love it when I'm out there. I feel like I'm with God at that time."

"Is there any way to make it so you don't have to do this other stuff?" I asked. "So you don't have to spend your life in this inauthentic way where you're always thinking about how much you dislike what you're doing?"

"Wow, I've never thought about making a living out of the orchard."

"Somebody's got to buy apples. Applesauce and apple pies have got to be made," I replied. "If you know what your bliss is, then it's just a matter of taking some of the risks that go with it. So why aren't you? Why restrict yourself in any way? How about giving yourself a chance?"

What I was trying to impart to this guy was, "You've got to love what you do, and you've got to do what you love." Everybody can do this. I don't think it matters too much what you're doing, but if you don't like it you have options. The first option you have is that you can take the risk to, as Joseph Campbell said, "Follow your bliss."

If you're not willing to take the risk, you can change your attitude. For example, this fellow could say, "All right. I'm going to work at the factory for only six or eight hours a day, then I'm going to get right out into my apple orchard." That's sort of what he was doing already, learning how to go to this assembly-line job that he had and not have such a negative attitude about it while still trying to make it fun.

You can change, even though you may feel that it's an uncomfortable process at first. You'll find that the people who care about you will support your consulting your inner signals and doing what it is that you know you have to do. You'll discover that you can live with a lot less, as long as you have joy inside you. The notion that you have to have a lot of stuff and a lot of accumulations in order to live happily is such a myth.

Success cannot happen for you if you don't take a risk, if you continue to do something you've always done because you've always done it. Then the only payoff you'll get for that is to defend your misery. It's like arguing for your limitations—the only thing you'll get are your limitations.

I don't believe that taking chances is risky at all, especially when it comes to doing what you love. If you picture yourself being successful and believe that it's going to work, and you won't let any other image into your brain, it will get stored away within you exactly the same as if you were out there working on it. And if you guide yourself by that image and won't let it go, you can't not make it happen. It's a law of the universe.

When you learn to see every obstacle as an opportunity to note what you need to do to shift and make some adjustments, risks stop being risks after a while. They only feel risky to people who are starting out on the path, who are beginning to find out how easy and how perfect all this is. The farther along you go, the fewer risks there are. When you become a no-limit person, it will not matter whether you fail, or whether somebody doesn't like it, or whether what you're doing "fits in." Those things are no longer a concern, and it's easier to simply be what you know you have to be.

It's smart to pursue an idea of something you want to be very much, even though you may be taking chances. And you need to do that even if you can't see how you're going to succeed yet. Although the road ahead may still be hidden, you must encourage yourself to take steps on it.

You really need to "just do it." That's the key word: *do.* If there's a pen sitting on a table in front of us, and I say to you, "All right, what I want you to do is try to pick up this pen," what's going to happen? You're going to do, not try!

So any kind of trying could be called "not picking up the pen." It's just not up yet. But then when you do pick it up, there's the pen up in the air. Trying is a human invention; it's the doing that is important. When you get out there and do what you love, you will be fulfilling the mission of your life.

Be a Beginner, and Let in the New

I once heard a story about a professor at a university who was an expert on Buddhism and East Asian religions, having written four or five books on the subject. He had always wanted to meet a particular Zen master who lived in India, so he went to meet this guru. The man was very old, peaceful, and kind, and the expert began talking to him about all the things that he knew about Zen and Buddhism and so on.

The master stopped him and asked, "Would you like a cup of tea?"

"Yes, that would be very nice."

The guru took a teacup and put it in a saucer. The man continued to talk about all the things he knew. The master began to pour the tea into the cup. The man kept on talking. Soon the cup was full, but the master continued to pour. The tea poured out of the cup and onto the saucer. As the man talked, the master still kept pouring. The tea was now going onto the floor and splashing on the man's feet.

Finally, the man said, "Excuse me, but the cup is full."

The master replied, "You are like the cup. You are so full of everything that you know, you don't have room to let anything else new in."

So many of us are like that teacup as well: We are so full of all the stuff we have learned, there's no more room to let anything else in. It's all just pouring out and going past us. If we could see that metaphor in ourselves, we'd understand that in the eyes of the beginner, there are millions of options; in the eyes of the expert, however, there are only one or two.

When it comes to finding your bliss, always come from the point of view of a beginner, never an expert. Imagine that you're going to learn how to play tennis. If you've never played it before, and someone hands you a racket and says, "Now try a drop shot this way," you'd be open. You are willing—"I'll do that." You'd try it this way and that, as the beginner has a thousand options available to them and would try everything.

If you talk to an expert about how to hit a drop shot, though, they know only one way. That's true not only in tennis but also in your business, in your relationships, and in everything in your life. You must stay a beginner as you move along your path. You can get so clogged up with what you know and with the negativity that goes with it

—all the rejection and judgment—because you have to deny or ignore other points of view in order to make sure that yours is the only one that ever gets heard. Thus, you don't have any room inside of you for something new, something exciting, something different, something that makes you grow.

Be wary of experts. Be wary of becoming one yourself, because then you limit yourself. By limiting yourself, your bliss or purpose can't find you. It's like an artery that's clogged up with cholesterol—nothing can flow through it, because it's too clogged. You've got to unclog yourself. The way to do so is by opening yourself up and advancing confidently and doing things that make sense to you, that make you feel good, that are of service to others, that are useful to other people.

In the Bhagavad Gita, it's said that one of the great lessons is in how much better it is to do your own work, even if you have to do it imperfectly, than it is to do somebody else's work perfectly. A lot of people don't get that, especially in Western culture. What it comes down to is understanding that if you are following your bliss or pursuing what you know you're about, then the real motivation is in just advancing confidently in the direction of your dreams. Even if you're not doing it as well as other people are doing it, or not doing it the way other people think you should be doing it, it's far more enlightening and much better for you as a person. Ultimately, it would serve many others in much greater ways for you to do your own thing blissfully than for you to do somebody else's work perfectly.

Remember: *Who you are is how you think. You become what you think about. As you think, so shall you be.* All of that is very important to keep reminding yourself.

Once you get in harmony, then what you have to give away is harmony. It becomes very clear what you have to do and why you're doing it. You can never pull away from that. If you're doing what somebody else thinks you should be doing, even if you're doing it perfectly, then inside where you do all your living, you are full of repugnance and hostility and disharmony. And if that's what you're thinking about, then that repugnance and hostility and disharmony is what expands. You can't be authentic unless you're following your bliss.

I discovered that for myself in so many of the jobs I've had over the years. It wasn't until I left them and really began to pursue what I loved, even if it was done less perfectly than what I was doing before, that I became authentic to myself. My thoughts, my spirit, my soul were now on bliss, and I became in harmony.

The Practicalities of Living Blissfully

People ask over and over again, "Is it practical to follow your bliss in a world that demands payment of mortgages and utility bills and insurance and so on?" The answer to that is, "If you think abundance, abundance will rain into your life." There's also the whole business of how addicted you are to your way of life, to the belief that you have to have the kinds of bills you have.

When Thoreau went to Walden, he wrote, "Simplicity, simplicity, simplicity! I say, let your affairs be as two or three, and not a hundred or a thousand." You have the choice to do this too. Work on reducing the amount of external pressures that are put on you in the way of expenses. Even though you may not think so, it's quite easy to return to simplicity. All you have to do is look back in your life to the times when it was simpler, when you didn't have to have somebody come in and do all the things you are paying people to do, when you were more in charge of your life. That's one option, which I personally am exercising more and more these days.

Another option is to believe that whatever level of income you have now, you're capable of having in the area of your own bliss—believe that and take the risks that go with it. The answer to whether or not you can pay your bills is in your own history. If you've always been a person who has paid your bills, then you're not going to suddenly become a person who doesn't. But if you've been a person who's never been responsible about paying your bills, then you probably won't pay them, even when you're following your bliss.

A lot of people will look at the whole history of their life and see that they've always been responsible, but then they get images in their mind of becoming irresponsible if they do something different. Instead of relying on that whole history, that whole long catalog of responsibility that has been your life, you come up with this horrible image that suddenly says, *I'm not going to be able to do those things any longer.*

I have found that when it comes to people who haven't been responsible in their life, it isn't that they're this way because they're not doing the kind of work they love or whatever; it is because that's what they have learned to do. That's what they have adopted as a lifestyle. They walk out on their bills, and they do it whether they are 14 or 30. They're broke when they retire. They blame life and circumstances and a bad break and all the things that so many folks blame for the conditions of their lives. On the other hand, people who have been responsible stay that way, no matter what.

One of the great things that I remember from reading about Gandhi's life was when he was asked by a group of reporters if he could summarize his philosophy in a few words. He quoted the great Vedic text, the Upanishads: "Renounce and enjoy!" By that, he didn't mean renounce the work you do, but renounce your attachment to how it comes out and just enjoy it. *Follow your bliss* means the same thing. And you'll only discover what your bliss is when you're unclogged from the negative things that keep it from coming into your life.

Always Look Inside

A lot of people think following your bliss is one of those things that falls in the category of "easy to say, very hard to do." My response to this is that it is difficult to do only if you believe it's difficult, like anything in life. Every single problem you face as a human being, whether it's in your job or relationships or finances or spirituality—whatever problem you have—the problem is in you. The faucet dripping is just a faucet dripping. That's all it is. The IRS audit that's coming up is just an IRS audit. That's what it is. Your children failing algebra is just your children failing algebra. That's what it is.

When it becomes a problem for you, somehow now it's yours. And when it becomes yours, it can only become yours through your mind. That's all you have to make it a problem: your mind. *Every single problem you face is an experience of your thinking.* You carry it around with you, you think about it, you go to sleep with it, whatever, but it's still in this invisible part of you, your mind.

Now, if you accept that the problem is in how you are processing it—that is, how you're using your mind—then you have to ask, "Where's the solution?" If you think the solution is in the faucet no longer dripping or your kid getting an A in algebra or the IRS telling you they've decided to give you a refund instead of an audit, then you're living an illusion.

The fact is that every problem is in your mind, and so is every solution—it cannot be that the solution is outside of yourself but the problem is inside of yourself. So make the choice right now to stop looking outside yourself for solutions to the problems that are inside you.

Think about this story: A man has lost his key. He's outside looking under his lamppost, when his friend comes along and asks if he can help. After they're looking for a while, the friend asks, "Where did you drop the key?"

"Oh, I dropped the key inside the house."

"Then what are you doing looking for it out here?"

The man replies, "There's no light in the house, so I decided to look under here where there's light."

Now, how much sense does it make to look outside for a key that you lost inside? The same analogy applies when you're looking outside for a solution to any problem. If you're looking for the solution under the lamppost when the problem is back inside, then you're just living an illusion. If you have a problem, it's because of how you think. The only way that you can ever fix a problem is by changing your thinking, and then you find the solution inside. If the IRS tells you that they're no longer going to audit you and in fact owe you money, and you say, "That's what made the problem go away," you are wrong. What made the problem go away is that you processed that event in a different way than you processed the previous one. I know this may be hard for you to accept, but the solution to any problem is always found in how you think.

In order to pursue your bliss, you have to first believe that this is something you can do. If you think you can't, that the circumstances of your life are such that you simply cannot do what you love and love what you do, then that's exactly what will expand for you. You might as well stop right here and put this book away, because you are not going to be able to pursue your bliss if you believe that this is only something I can say, not something you can do.

You must believe that *There is a possibility that given the circumstances of my life, I can also be blissfully doing what I love and loving what I do. I can do that.* The solution to being able to do it is inside you, just like the problem of not doing it is inside you. Never look for things outside you to change in order for you to become happier.

There are three key points to consider here:

1. You must believe that following your bliss is a possibility. This means examining (or reexamining) your resistance to doing what you love. What is it that is keeping you from doing what you love and loving what you do, independent of success, performance, achievement, and acquisitions?

I'll guarantee you that if you interview 1,000 people, 999 of them are going to say, "It's impractical. I can't do that. I made a decision a long time ago to do what I'm doing now. Even though I don't like it, this is what I'm stuck with. My family wouldn't support me. I can't take the risks to do it."

When I look back at my own life before I did what I loved and loved what I was doing, here's what jumps out at me: Even though I was very good at being a professor and counselor, I was doing other people's work perfectly at the expense of doing what I wanted to do imperfectly. Because I hadn't been a writer. I hadn't been out on my own. I hadn't been pursuing my passion.

I was going back and forth to work every day in drill—
life had become very routine, very dull, and stultifying to
my creative impulses. This happens when you get on the
right path; the time comes when you can no longer tolerate what you don't want to do. Now, some people have no
problem with a routine existence. They keep repeating the
kinds of things that they are doing over and over again,
in the name of getting a gold watch someday or whatever.
Well, that was not for me.

Instead, I got to thinking about what a blissful life
would be like. I began to get a picture of myself getting
up in the morning and, instead of getting dressed, going
to my typewriter in my pajamas. To me, going to work in
my pajamas was a great image—I loved envisioning myself
rolling out of bed and going to my typewriter, doing what
I wanted to do and being in control. I began to visualize myself doing all this, writing on my own schedule, on
my own terms, and getting my work out there. I began to
see myself doing that. When you change your thoughts,
or the pictures you see, you end up changing around the
Divine part of you.

The more I saw myself doing all this, it began to become a reality for me. The only thing that I hadn't done
yet was allow my physical self to pursue the dream I had.
I found myself getting more and more discontented as I
drove back and forth to work on the Long Island Expressway every day. Then one day, I'd had enough. I got to the
university and went right into the dean's office, and I told
her that I was resigning. Even though I had a very prom-
ising future as a professor, I simply could not do it any
longer. So I said I'd be leaving at the end of the semester.

When I drove home, I experienced the most peaceful
moment I can ever remember in my life related to work. As
I went along on the expressway, the traffic was different,

the sky was different, the interior of my car was different. I felt so excited, so full of joy, knowing that I was finally going to exercise the kind of freedom I'd always wanted in my life. It truly wasn't about money. It was about going out there and taking a chance. As soon as I began to examine the risks, I said, "I can handle them."

2. There's no scarcity of opportunity to make a living at what you love. There's only a scarcity of resolve to make it happen. That's very important. Whatever it is that you love, whatever it is that's your bliss, know that there are people out there someplace making a living off of it. The absence of that resolve comes from fear: *I will probably fail; this isn't going to work out; other people will laugh at me.*

Remember, other people's opinions are just that. You've got to get to the point where you're not directing your life or motivating yourself based on anything that anybody out there might say or not say to you. Why should you listen to somebody else's editorial opinion about how you should be living your life? The risk of running into disapproval is no longer a risk when you're able to see disapproval for what it is. It doesn't say anything about you when somebody else approves or disapproves of what you do or don't do. It's about them.

And again, when you move along the path of enlightenment, you discover there's no such thing as failure, as everything you do produces a result. The question isn't whether or not you're going to produce results, but what you're going to do with the results you produce. If you go to hit a golf ball off a tee and it dribbles off to the side, you haven't failed—you've produced a result.

You can do a lot of things with the result you've produced. You could say, "See? I told you, I can't hit golf balls. I'm not very athletic. This isn't the kind of person I am.

I'm not talented like this. I've always been that way. I can't help it. That's my nature." You can use all these excuses to never hit a golf ball again. Or you can say, "I better try that again. Watch how I swing this time!" And you practice this again and again . . . and this is the stuff champions are made of.

You don't fail at anything—you produce results at everything.

3. If you refuse to change what you do, then practice loving it every day. You might not want to give up your job, and that's very sensible in a lot of cases. It is absolutely within reason to make this choice.

There's a wonderful Zen koan that goes like this: "Before enlightenment: chopping wood, carrying water. After enlightenment: chopping wood, carrying water." Enlightenment has nothing to do with whether you chop wood or carry water. We are all going to chop wood and carry water in some way. The enlightened among us know how to reframe our thinking toward what we're doing.

If you don't want to change what you do in order to pursue your bliss, then change your attitude toward what you do. If you're going in to work every day and thinking about how much you dislike what you're doing, and you know that what you think about is what expands, then what's going to expand is your dislike.

The key to following your bliss is this: *You have to fall in love with what you do. Then, sell that love.* You don't sell what you do; you don't sell your product. You fall in love with what you do, much like you fall in love with your significant other and your children. What you're going to sell is that love for what you do. You sell that enthusiasm, that excitement, that joy, that fulfillment—that exquisite, loving, peaceful, serene feeling about what you do. This is exactly what I do.

I don't go out and sell my books; I love what I've written, and that's what I sell. I sell that enthusiasm, that excitement, that authentic feeling of making a difference. When you're able to sell the love, enthusiasm, and excitement you feel, then it doesn't make any difference what product you have. If you are a dentist and love what you're doing and you're selling that love, then you're going to create an enthusiastic, loving practice. People are going to want to come to you to have their teeth cleaned. Or if you are selling widgets and you have the enthusiasm and excitement, and you are authentic about it, then people are going to want to be around that love. You sell the love.

Say you're doing a job that you think is routine, but you've now made a decision that you're going to keep doing it because you've only got 10 more years until you retire. What you do here is change around your attitude and look for the excitement in your job. Don't go in there every day saying, "Ugh, I can't believe I have to do this." Instead, say, "I'm getting paid to do this thing here. This is what I'm producing. As a result of producing this, I'm going to be helping so many people."

If you're working on an assembly line affixing bolts to things, put those bolts on with integrity and enthusiasm and excitement. You know that bolt is going to save lives because without it, a door would fall off or whatever—love that. Feel good about it if that job is what you want to do. If not, then you have to change what you do. You only have two choices here: You either change what you do, or you change how you process what you do. You look for the good in it. That can be done in any job out there, or anything you have chosen to do.

What Are You For?

Understand that whatever you're currently against can be restated and rethought so as to promote abundance in your life. You have to grasp this very simple premise: *Everything you're against weakens you; everything you're for empowers you*. What you want to do is try not to be against anything. If you're against the conditions in your job, and all you do is talk about the people you dislike or the behaviors you notice in other people that offend you and make you upset, try to stop yourself. Remember that all the things you're against are weakening you, and you want to follow your bliss.

If your boss is cantankerous and nasty and abusive toward you and you're against that, then you become cantankerous and abusive yourself. You become part of cantankerousness and abusiveness; you are it, and it is you. Of course you don't want that, so how can you take something you're against and reframe it to promote abundance in your life? Well, what are you *for*?

You are for having a harmonious relationship with this person. So focus on that: *This is what I'm for. This is what I'm going to create because my boss's behavior isn't what is making me upset. How I process his behavior is the problem, so I'm going to process it differently. I am going to see his behavior as where he is on his path. This is what he is doing. I'm not going to process it in a way that is going to pit me against it any longer. I'm going to do things to defuse his nastiness. I'm going to teach him that he can't get to me with that. Because what I'm for is harmony in this relationship. I never move away from what I'm for. I treat the conflict that is created there as just an opportunity for me to learn how to go past it.*

Always keep in mind what you're for. Every time your boss behaves in a negative way, instead of joining him in his anger and hatred and bitterness, shift your consciousness to, *What am I for? I'm for harmony. How can I send some harmony to this guy?*

Have you ever tried to pick a fight with somebody who doesn't want to fight? It's really difficult. It's very challenging indeed to have an argument with somebody who refuses to argue. By shifting away from what you are against to what you are for, that's what you become with your boss. The more you think about what you are for, you become empowered. You convert that relationship from one of anger and hostility to one of joy. In just a matter of days, you can do that. You can actually give him a gift.

All the things that you find yourself so resistant to doing, if it's tough for you to do inside, then that's the clue. You must go ahead with it. Once you find yourself shifting all that around, you restate what you want from what you're against to what you're for. You'll find that bliss is your reward.

JOURNAL EXERCISE

As you've been reading the last two chapters, you may have been wondering, *How do I know what my bliss is?* If so, the first thing to understand is that you know what it *isn't.* You know what doesn't light the fire of passion in your heart, for sure. That's no problem.

I included a display quote from Oprah Winfrey at the beginning of Part III of this book, and here's the rest of what she has to say on the topic:

How do you know whether you're on the right path? The same way you know when you're not: You feel it. Each of us has a personal call to greatness—and because yours is as unique to you as your fingerprint, no one can tell you what it is . . .

Your life is speaking to you every day, all the time—and your job is to listen up and find the clues. Passion whispers to you through your feelings, beckoning you toward your highest good. Pay attention to what makes you feel energized, connected, stimulated—what gives you your juice. Do what you love, give it back in the form of service, and you will do more than succeed. You will triumph.

In your journal, write down how you feel about these words. When your life speaks to you, what does it say?

CHAPTER 11

CULTIVATE YOUR OWN GARDEN

One day I came home from school and asked my mother, "What's a scurvy elephant?"

She said, "I don't know. I have no idea what that is."

"Well, I heard the teacher saying that Wayne Dyer was a scurvy elephant in the classroom."

My mother got my teacher on the phone, who said, "No, I didn't say that at all. I said he was a *disturbing element* in the classroom."

Yes, I have always been that scurvy elephant. There's a wonderful line from a letter E. E. Cummings wrote that says it all to me: "To be nobody-but-yourself—in a world which is doing its best, night and day, to make you everybody else—means to fight the hardest battle which any human being can fight; and never stop fighting."

I think that sums up what my beliefs are more than almost anything in the world. It is about just going out there and being the person you want to be without any feelings of being manipulated by anyone else. Not being someone who feels they have to conform and fit in and do what everybody else thinks they should be doing is perhaps the greatest freedom you can have. There are a lot of people who think that freedom comes from external motivation, such as being able to make a lot of money, receiving numerous accolades, getting the adulation of all their friends, or winning a football game or a tennis match—they think these are the markers of success. As we've learned, these things don't mean that at all.

Remember, happiness is an inner concept. You can't get it. You can search for it forever, and you'll never find it. I'm sure you've heard the saying, "Wherever I go, there I am." This means that you've always got yourself to deal with, so you should only be concerned with consulting your inner signals.

I think perhaps there's the notion that books by people like me are instructing readers to be selfish. That is actually the furthest thing in the world from anything I believe or endorse, and I certainly don't even know how to behave that way in my own life. I'm not a proponent of selfishness or using other people for your own ends. If I were, my book titles would have been along the lines of *How to Use Other People as Stepping-Stones to Your Own Self-Actualization.* That isn't what I believe at all.

To me, the greatest priority in life is the ability to enjoy it. People who know how to do this—how to take each day they are alive and go through it with joy—are operating in the least selfish way that can be.

Take someone who knows how to enjoy living, who knows how to take any circumstance in their life and turn it into something positive, who is never down or a burden to anybody else—well, that is an enlightened human being. When you encounter a person like that, you will never find them manipulating others or trying to sacrifice their life for other people, or worrying what everybody else is thinking about them, or anything else like that.

This is a very important concept to get into your head. When you get yourself to the point where you can take delight in each day that you're alive, you will never be anybody else's burden. You won't even know *how* to be anybody else's trouble or burden. Then when you are that shining light, when you are enjoying your life, you are doing something unselfish, and without even trying. You're helping other people by setting your own example of what it means to be a no-limit person.

Live and Let Live

As I've mentioned already, awakened people look for solutions, never for problems. They tend to be focused on, *Okay, these are the conditions. Let's see what can be done to make them work better.*

For example, I encountered a very rude flight attendant a while back who seemed to have forgotten her positive customer-service skills. For some reason she was angry with me about where my bag was to go. There was a time when I would have responded with disability and used anger back, which would only have served to create more anger. But I have evolved along my path of enlightenment, so I knew instantly that this was her problem, not mine. After she barked at me, I replied, "Boy, you must be having a really tough day. You've probably been flying all over the country, huh?"

She immediately softened and said, "Oh yeah, I'm going on two days without sleep."

"Well, why don't you just relax? I'll get this thing put away," I told her, and everything was fine.

This illustrates how even a seemingly small event can become an example of a solution-oriented way, rather than a problem-oriented way, of dealing with something. More important, the reason I was able to defuse the situation is because I didn't own it, not for one second. I understood that this was her stuff; it had nothing to do with me. In any situation that you encounter in life, you must always keep in mind that you're looking for *solutions*. You're not looking to be right or to win.

This reminds me of something that happened when my daughter Tracy was young. My nephews were staying with us, and one of them was sleeping on a mattress in the living room. When he got up, I said, "Tom, you've got to do something with that mattress."

"I think the best thing to do is throw it in Tracy's room," he replied. That worked for him. He threw it in there Monday, threw it in there Tuesday, threw it in there Wednesday.

At that point, my daughter reached the limit of her tolerance. She wanted to talk to me about why he had done that.

I told her, "Honey, look for a solution, don't look for a problem. Monday, Tuesday, and Wednesday are over. You taught him to throw the mattress in your room by the fact that you put up with it. So what is it you want to say to him?"

"'Keep your mattress out of my room.'"

"Okay, then go tell him that."

She did, and Tom said, "Fine." He threw it in my room, and I threw him out. I'm kidding, of course, but we did ultimately come up with a solution that worked for all of us.

Did you ever notice how hard it is to be in conflict with somebody who doesn't want to be dragged down, who doesn't want to be unhappy, who doesn't want to be mad? They're not interested in being right, so conflict disappears pretty quickly. Such individuals are motivated by their need for truth, for beauty, for morality, for individuality. These are very important concepts to them. Although you don't tend to meet many people like that, you can meet them anywhere—in a Dairy Queen, in a cab, in a waiting room. They don't have to be philosophers or anybody who's achieved anything special, but when you're around them, you know it.

They're unafraid yaysayers who have a great deal of love for everything that is alive. They focus on the present moment and are all about the now. They're not obsessed with where they used to be or where they're going to be. Worry and guilt are not part of their lives. They have the quality of being able to say to themselves, *This is what has meaning for me, and I have to do it because I believe it's right, even if I fly in the face of criticism from everybody else down the line.*

You may wonder, *How can I achieve these qualities in myself? How can I live more fully?* The answer, of course, is you just do it.

I think about a guy who lived a few centuries ago, named Voltaire. He wrote a marvelous book called *Candide,* which is really the journey of a man and his partner looking for themselves. The conclusion they came to is found in the last line of the book: "We must learn to cultivate our own garden." They were looking for riches everywhere, and all they ever found was frustration. The thing they learned was how to cultivate their own garden.

To me, that's one of the most insightful things ever written. You must learn to cultivate your own garden and keep your nose out of everybody else's. If they want to grow rutabagas in it, if they want to use a different kind of fertilizer than you do, if they want to have weeds in it, that's really none of your business. The important thing is that yours is the way you want it to be. Learn how to take what it is that you have and enjoy it and make your life work on your terms, cultivating for yourself a sense of purpose and a mission for yourself. This is one of the greatest secrets you can learn: Get your own garden in order. Grow what you want to grow, and stop focusing on everybody else's.

One of the toughest things for people to understand is something I learned from Tibetan Buddhism: "Everything in the universe is exactly as it should be." Think of that. Whatever is out there is supposed to be there. The evidence for this is: it is. That's all. That doesn't mean you can't change things. If you can change things, then do so, instead of getting mad at the world for the way it is or blaming the mirror for what it reflects. Accept it, and *then* do what you can to improve it.

You have to get your mind off of judgment, though. Think about this: A couple of elderly folks walk down to the beach and say, "Look at those kids. They hardly wear any clothes when they go to the beach. They're throwing Frisbees and they have their dogs over there, just making such a racket." All this is is judgment. They're looking at the world and saying, "I don't accept it for what it is. I want it to be different."

Then the young people see the elderly folks and say, "Look at those old fogies with their wrinkles. They don't wear anything modern. They're always mad at us and don't have any fun at all." This is more judgment, not looking at the world as everything in it is exactly as it should be.

Instead of going by the old adage of "Live and let live," we judge others. We wish things would be different, something other than what they are. Rather than looking at the world through judgmental eyes, ask yourself the question that philosophers like to pose: *Do you see the world as it is, or as you are?* If you see the world as you are, then you want it to be the way you think it should be. If you see the world as it is, then you can improve it.

The Power of Forgiveness

Back in 1974, I had a phenomenal experience. I have told this story many times over the years, but it seems to have a profound effect every time I do, so I'd like to share it again now.

I had been searching for my father from the time I was eight years old, and I had dreams about him all the time. I'd never even seen this man, and anything I'd ever heard about him had been most unflattering. It seems that he was extremely cruel to everybody he had ever met, and his life was an ignominious one in almost every way.

And yet there was something inside of me . . . there was an anger, there was a pain, there was a suffering. It made me want to talk to this man and find out, "How do you abandon three children? How do you leave a woman and never pay her any child support? How do you use alcohol to destroy yourself? How do you beat somebody up and rape them, and create a pregnancy that way, and other stories I've heard sort of backhand because it was too painful for my mother to talk about? How do you do all of this? Where does it come from?"

I wanted to know because I thought somehow his leaving could have been courageous. Maybe he simply couldn't stay and face things, maybe he loved us all too much . . . who knows? If you don't know, you just wonder and continue to think about it, which is what I did. My two brothers couldn't have cared less about any of it. My oldest brother, Jim, had some memory of our father, but my brother Dave didn't. Neither one of them was at all interested in my quest.

I must tell you this, because it really is relevant: When your life matches up with what you believe you are here for, suddenly—and it is suddenly—your purpose begins to own you, and you get on such a fast track that nothing can stop you. Your purpose, whatever it may be, can become related to anything in your life, and it is magnificent. And when you live it, it starts to own you. That's the only way I can say it.

This business about my father—and the anguish, the pain, the suffering, the dreams, and so on—carried on even years after I found out that he had died. A distant cousin told me that he had passed away in New Orleans and his body had been shipped to Biloxi, Mississippi, and that was all the information anybody had.

In 1974, I was a professor at St. John's University in New York, and I also had the opportunity to earn some extra money by helping out a fellow educator. I was asked to go down to this college in Columbus, Mississippi, to make sure they were in compliance with the Civil Rights Act of 1964. I was to spend two days observing, sitting in on classes and the like, and then send a report back. When I found out I'd be only four hours from Biloxi, I decided it was time to see if I could find out the answers to some of the questions I'd had for decades.

I had flown into Columbus, so I went and rented a car when I was done with my work at the college. They gave me one that was so new it had only eight-tenths of a mile on the odometer. I wondered, *How the hell did they get it here? I mean, what is this new car doing in Columbus, Mississippi?* I didn't understand that at all, but I kind of made a mental note of it.

I went to put my seat belt on. In those days, they didn't have shoulder straps but just went across your lap. I reached down to get the seat belt, but I couldn't get it out. I literally had to take the seat out of the car to get at the seat belt, because even in 1974, I wasn't going to drive without a seat belt.

I was able to get the seat belt out, and it was all wrapped in plastic. As I unwrapped it, I discovered a business card that said: CANDLELIGHT INN—BILOXI, MISSISSIPPI. I put the card in my pocket and didn't think any more of it.

I set out on my drive down to Biloxi, picked up this guy hitchhiking who was a migrant worker, and took a little side trip to drop him off. It was a quarter to five on a Friday afternoon when I arrived at the outskirts of Biloxi. I went to a gas station, found a phone booth, and looked through the yellow pages. I figured I'd call the three cemeteries that were listed to find out if my father was buried here.

I called the first one, and there was no answer. I called the second one and got a busy signal. I called the third one, and after it rang for a while, someone did pick up. I said, "Hello, my name is Wayne Dyer, and I'm calling to find out if a Melvin Lyle Dyer is buried there."

The guy said he'd check and went away for the longest time. He finally came back and said yes, someone by that name was buried there.

My heart was beating right out of my chest—*ba-doom, ba-doom, ba-doom.* It felt like the end of a very long journey. I said, "All right, now how do I get there?"

"It's very easy," he replied. "We are on the grounds of the Candlelight Inn."

I reached into my pocket and pulled out the business card; sure enough, it was the same place. So I went there, and found my father's grave. I stood there and talked and talked to this man I had never met before.

I had this long dialogue with him in which I forgave him for everything that he had done—to my mother, to my brother Dave, and especially to my brother Jim, to whom he had done a lot of horrible things. I wasn't thinking about forgiveness, or how important it was, or whether I should do it, or anything like that. But that's what happened. I spent about two and a half hours there, and tears were streaming down my face the whole time. I took the time to forgive my father, and it changed my life.

I want to tell you that whatever you have going on in the way of animosity, bitterness, anguish, or pain toward any other human being on our planet—whoever they are and whatever they've done—if your reaction is one of toxic bitterness, it will never let go of you. Forgiveness is the greatest motivator in the world. If you are hanging on to anything painful or hurtful toward anyone or anything, I speak from personal experience when I say that you've got to let go of it all.

You don't have to do what I did—you don't have to visit any graves or make any phone calls, nor do you have to let anybody else know that you're doing it. In your heart, all you have to do is purify yourself in such a way that you simply say, "Love is forgiving." Now, that last part can be both two words and one word. When it's one word, it's *forgiving*, which is what we've been discussing here. But it's also *for giving*, so it's a gift, meaning that you don't ask anything back of it.

After my experience in Biloxi, my whole life became so clear and focused, and where I was going became so evident. I left there and immediately outlined *Your Erroneous Zones*. And I've never had another dream about my father since then. I've never had a moment's anguish of any kind toward him or anything that he has done. I am now completely at peace with him, and I send him love, wherever he is. It's all okay.

In fact, I've come to think of Melvin Lyle Dyer as my greatest teacher. Without those experiences that were the result of some of the things he had done, my opportunity to help so many people and to create wonderful things for others, including myself, would never, ever have materialized. I see that, and I see a need for that, and I believe in it. And I also want to say to you that whatever you've got inside you, it is not the result of what anybody else put there. It's the result of what you decide to have inside you. It all comes back to choice.

Send Love to Everyone

Take a moment to think about all the people in your life with whom you have any conflict. If it's about something that happened with your mother when you were two, if it's your neighbor, if it's your boyfriend, whoever it is, list them in your mind, from the person with whom you have the most trouble to the one who just annoys you. Then send them all love.

See, it's easy to send love to the folks who do the things they're supposed to do, who are nice to you and smell good. That's not a test of love. When Christ was on the cross and someone threw a spear into his rib, his reaction was: "Father, forgive them, for they do not know what they are doing." When people who claim to be Christians tell me whom they hate and whom they don't, I say, "You're a Christian because that is the title you have placed on yourself, but you're not Christlike." And that's the test—to be Christlike, not a Christian. Being part of the orthodoxy is easy—anybody can do that. All they have to do is call themselves Christian and go to church on Sunday. But that is not Christlike.

Commit to working on this: every time you find negativity in your life, practice sending out love to that person, even if somebody is being really nasty to you. You can practice with something as small as dealing with aggressive drivers, and then move on to bigger things, like when someone uses cutthroat tactics at work or a friend betrays your confidence. Ultimately, you'll make that a way of life.

As you send out love, love will come back into your life in greater and greater amounts. And you become free, because the hate you harbor is a poison that's worse than any cancer. It will continue to eat at you until you can send love. Until you are able to do this, you won't be able to experience optimal, awakened living without limits.

I have to practice this in my own life as well. I had someone who was suing me, and they wanted to take advantage of my position in life and make some money off it for themselves. I was so mad about it: *How could this person do that? Who was this attorney who took this case, and how do they live with themselves?* I fought it, but all I got out of it was being right, a big legal bill, and months and months of anguish and pain. When I began to send this person love, I came to understand that this was all about them.

I realized that some Eastern philosophies would view what I went through as a test to see what I was made out of. There was a lesson in there, and I needed to try to find the blessing in the pain. I started doing that, and before I knew it, the lawsuit was dropped. I became much more productive, my writing improved, and I began to feel better as a human being. My secretary even said, "You seem so much lighter now. It's almost like you were walking on air when all of that stuff was finally sent away."

There are people who owe me money and haven't paid it back over the years, and it used to make me really mad: *How dare this person? I loaned them money, but they ended up just taking it. That's stealing!* I've now dropped that anger and have even sent those individuals copies of my books. I let it go. I don't believe in not paying your bills, and I personally pay mine as soon as they come in. But some people are in a different place, and I don't want to be owned by their behavior. If I'm upset because they refuse to pay money back to me, their refusal is the source of my upset. I am allowing somebody else's behavior to control my life at this moment. I don't want that.

If you're in a similar situation, know that there's only one way out: forgiveness. You've got to let it go. You don't have to forget; you just have to forgive. You don't have to call them up or send them notes if that's not what you want to do. Just let it go—when you do, that's called *nonattachment.* You are no longer attached to this person or their behavior, and when you're not attached to it, you're then free to be the creative genius you are. Nonattachment is a principle that works magnificently.

Here's another example from an attorney friend of mine who's going through a horrible divorce. His wife wants half of his law practice, along with the children and all his money. Apparently, she had an affair and then he found out. They once had a great marriage, but now they're going through all this hatred. He was sitting across from me at this beautiful restaurant, and I could see the anguish in him. He was full of so much pain that he'd seemingly aged 10 years in 4 months.

He wanted to spend the whole night telling me how right he was and how wrong she was. He kept saying that she had no right to do this. "How dare she treat me this way? Do you know that she actually brought this man over to my own home? Wayne, what do you think?"

I said, "You need to be right, don't you?"

"No, I don't. Anyway, what do you think of what I've told you? Does she have a right to do any of that?"

"Yes."

"What do you mean, 'yes'?"

"She did it," I explained. "You can't undo what she's done."

"Well, what do you think I should do?"

"I think you should forgive her."

"I already did," he assured me. "I already told her that."

"No, you don't have to tell her anything to forgive her," I said. "Instead, let it go. What are you defending? You're so racked with pain that you can hardly get up in the morning, and your practice is going to hell. You're depressed. Your blood pressure is going up. You're not eating. You're losing weight much too quickly. You're suffering—and you're suffering because you're not willing to forgive her.

"It has nothing to do with her. This is your test. And I wish I could get inside your head and let you know how important it is to send her love, even though she behaved in a way that you find so atrocious. You have to do this because otherwise you won't survive. It's clear that you're killing yourself right now. It happens to be a slow process; it's going to take a little while. If you want to stop killing yourself, then sooner or later you're going to have to forgive her, so why not choose sooner and just do it? You don't have to stay married to her or anything."

"What about the money and all that?"

"How much does she want?"

He whispered it, and I said, "Give her that and a little more."

"What!"

I said, "Don't worry, it will come back to you. But give her more, and pay it in advance. Let her know that you are not interested in being married anymore, but you're also not going to carry this around any longer. Then practice forgiveness—you will find a serenity and a beauty and a peace in your life that you never thought could be there before. It will be right there for you; all you have to do is forgive. All you have to do is understand that she's a human being and she made a mistake. You haven't.

"Yes, she got caught, and you didn't do anything wrong or whatever it is—let all that go. You will find so much enrichment in your life because now you won't be using up your present moments to convince yourself how right you are. It won't be important anymore. Being right is not necessary any longer; being happy is. And that's what you'll carry around inside you."

Like my friend, you must remember that everything you need to be completely happy, successful, and fulfilled, you already have. All you have to do is let go of that which owns you.

Think of yourself as holding on to prison bars and screaming, "Let me out! Let me out!" Then you look to the left and to the right of the bars, and it's all open space. You turn around, and it's all open space back there. Because of your tunnel vision, you've been looking straight ahead at the only way you know how to do things.

All those entrapments have made you feel like you're locked in a cell, but look to the left and look to the right and look behind you. You are holding on to bars in a cell that is open—all you have to do is let go and walk around them. In the process, you can become a fully liberated person, with no limits in sight.

JOURNAL EXERCISE

In your journal, write about the people you need to forgive, and how you can do this. In what other ways can you work on cultivating your own garden—that is, looking to a future that is free and clear of the negativity that's been holding you back?

CHAPTER 12

NINE QUESTIONS TO HELP SPARK CHANGE

Change is such a paradox: Everything is changing and nothing is changing at the same time. Everything is and everything isn't at the same time. The universe and all of us in it are constantly evolving, but still within the confines of what the universe is.

I look at it like this. If you were to stand back and gaze at a picture on your wall, and I asked you if it was complete, you'd say that of course it was. But if you then took the most powerful microscope you could find and looked down inside the picture, you'd discover that within each little bit of paint, there are whole universes in there that have nothing to do with the universe on the other side of the painting or across from it. And there are little bugs in the purples and the greens and the blues—there are bacteria in there, and if you look within each life-form, there are more life-forms. As you go farther and farther inside, you'd see that within this completed picture there are trillions of cells, endlessly going in that direction. It's also endless going the other direction. The universe doesn't end; it just goes on.

I think if we could all get back far enough and see the universe as a picture, we'd find that it's already complete. It's all total; it's all whole. It has to be. And yet within it, if we were to break it down, we'd see that so much is happening. We can change and do anything we want within the completeness of the whole thing—we have free will and we don't have free will at the same time. We have change that is taking place, but we look at the picture and that's not changing at all.

Now, what does it take for people to get the big picture? What does it take to get them to make real and lasting change? The answer to that is different for everybody. For some people, they need a therapist and a support group, they need to go to a rehabilitation center, they need to read 400 books, and they need to have everything reinforced over and over again in order to change. That's the way some people are wired, and that's all fine. If that's how your internal circuitry works, then by all means, go with it.

I, on the other hand, am not that kind of person. I make decisions instantaneously about what my life is going to be or not be. When I was about 14 or 15 years old, for instance, I tried coffee. It was bitter. It tasted funny, like chemicals that I didn't want. I said to my mother and my brothers, "I will never drink coffee in my life." That was many, many years ago. I tasted it, made up my mind, declared my intention, and have never had a cup of coffee since then. People offer it to me, but I know that I don't want that bitter taste in my mouth. I don't want that caffeine. I *know* that.

This is how I am able to make change, but it doesn't mean that's the right way or the best way. I can sit here with great confidence and say I won't be drinking coffee.

I can say that for certain. I can speak with certainty about a lot of things in my life, that I won't be overweight, that I'll stay away from cigarettes, that I will stay in shape, and all those kinds of things. For others, it's a daily struggle. The important thing is that you know yourself, but you also know you have the power to do whatever you need to do to improve your life.

As we come to the end of this book, I'd like to leave you with a series of questions to ponder, in order to guide you on your way to a no-limit life:

1. If you suddenly discovered that you had six months to live, how would you change your life? What would you do? If you knew that six months from now it was going to be all over for you, what would you do differently? Would you stay in the same job, for example? Would you want to keep things as they are, or would you get out and try something new?

This is a good question, because the future is promised to no one. Each of us has only so much time, and it goes by in the blink of an eye. Of course, you probably have much more than six months, but even if you have several decades, your time here is still short. So what do you want to do with it? Do you want to make a difference in the world? Do you want to go out and help other people? Do you want to end some of the real problems we have on this planet? Do you want to try things you've never tried before? Do you just want to have more fun or laugh more?

Whatever answers popped up for you are very telling. The advice I have for you is to take the risk to do whatever you want to do. Go for it!

2. Who would you choose to live with, if you could live with anyone else in the world and had no history with those you've lived with up until now? Imagine that your life started right this minute, and you haven't lived with anyone yet. Who would you choose to live with? Would you pick the person you're in a relationship with now? Would you change some things?

Then ask yourself why you aren't surrounding yourself with the kinds of people you'd love to be with. Do you have to be trapped? Can you teach those you do love to be excited and happy and alive and creative, and to make life pleasant? What about the people who are complainers and whiners and try to bring you down each day—can you teach them to be positive?

This may sound silly, but every morning when I go to shave, I look in the mirror and say, "Nobody on this planet is going to ruin this day for you. Nobody." Even if somebody's going to cut me off on the freeway, even if he's planning, "I'm gonna get Wayne Dyer," he is *not* going to get my day. If someone talks back to me or doesn't want to do what I want or gives me a bad attitude, no matter—this is my day. I don't care who they are or how much I love them, I'm not going to let anybody have this day. After you begin practicing such a mind-set, before long you get good at being someone you and others like being around.

Know that if you're living out of a sense of obligation instead of choice, you are a slave. Don't stay with a person you've been with simply because you've been with them for a long time, and that is the only reason. If you're doing something because you're "supposed to" do it, because everybody else is telling you to, then you are not listening to your inner signals. Relationships based on obligation lack dignity; relationships based on choice, freedom, and love have all the dignity in the world.

3. Where would you choose to live if you had no awareness of where you've lived up until now? Again, imagine that you have no history of living in a particular place. Take a look at that big globe we call our home and ask yourself, *Where would I like to be?*

Then ask yourself, *What is it that keeps me from being there? Is it fear? Is it the concern that I won't make it? That I'll fail or fall on my face?* Remind yourself that fears are only thought processes. If you're making it here and doing well and feeling a sense of success, you can do that anywhere. So why not be where you choose to be rather than staying in a particular place because your great-grandparents landed there as immigrants or whatever?

4. How much sleep do you think you would get if you had no clock and no ability to measure time? Do you think you'd get 8 hours, 10 hours, whatever it is? Do you think you'd spend a third of your life unconscious?

Studies have been done on this type of thing. They've put people in underground bunkers for weeks at a time, taking away all references to time, just having a dull light in there and meals served at no particular time or anything. The subjects could sleep whenever they wanted, and the amount they got was monitored. You know how much people slept when they didn't know what time of the day it was? It averaged out to 4.4 hours per day.

It turns out that a big part of sleep is simply not knowing what do with your life. You might think to yourself, *Why don't I get up earlier in the morning? Eh, what the hell am I going to do if I get up? I guess I'll stay here and sleep some more.* Or, *It's 10 o'clock, so I must be sleepy.*

I am not suggesting that you should try to deprive yourself of sleep if you need it, of course. Rather, this is just an exercise in trying to get you to tune in to your own needs rather than running your life according to clocks, calendars, and the like.

5. When and how much would you eat if there were no such thing as mealtimes? How many people eat three meals a day because that's what they're served or that's what they're supposed to do? Or operate on the notion that *I'm not hungry now, but I'll be hungry later, so I might as well gobble all this food down?*

See what I'm getting at? I'm talking about learning to live your life based on internal, rather than external, signals. So this is a good question to ask yourself before taking yourself off any schedule you might've put yourself on.

Most people put way too much food in their body without even thinking about it, particularly of the unhealthy, processed, or sugary variety. If weight is any kind of a problem for you, don't mindlessly eat everything on your plate. Instead, after thoroughly chewing each bite, ask yourself, *Do I want any more food? And does my body demand any more food?* Once the answer is no, stop. You've had enough.

6. What would you do if there were no such thing as money? What would you be doing in your life on a daily basis? What kinds of activities would you engage in? It's an interesting question. Are you doing what you're doing because it's earning you a living or you've got good benefits or you've only got a few more years until you retire or the like?

If you're doing something you don't like for a paycheck, what would you rather be doing? What do you like to do more than anything else? When you come up with the answer to that question, you can figure out a way to make that into a living. Know that whatever you're interested in doing, you can also earn a living at it. There are more than seven billion people on this planet, so there's going to be a demand for anything you do. Anything.

I dislike vocational-counseling guidance, mostly because it tries to trap people. It says, "Study this, go after that, take inventory, let's see how many things you like and dislike and then get that job and stay there for 50 years," instead of saying, "The sky's the limit."

You can do *anything*. You can work at whatever you want. And if you don't like your job or don't want to do it anymore, you can stop doing it. Try being a sportscaster or an artist or a musician or whatever it may be. Rather than doing things because you're supposed to make money at them, do them because they give you inner peace.

7. How old would you be if you didn't know how old you were? (This is Satchel Paige's question.) Would you be old? Middle-aged? Young? Then go ahead and forget how old you are. Because the aging process itself is in fact a direct result of attitude and what you believe about your life.

It's my contention that the no-limit person can choose when to die—they can do even that. I know a man who, the day before he turned 97 years old, announced, "Living is no longer what I want for myself. Tomorrow I die." Sure enough, the next day he lay down, closed his eyes, and that was it. There have also been chronicles of indigenous tribes whose chiefs were able to do the very same thing.

You can live as long as you choose to, and you can live as fully as you choose to. Look at people like George Bernard Shaw and Will Durant, who lived well into their 90s. Like them, you can still be productive and fulfilled and excited as you age, or you can be old and tired and complaining.

So what choice will you make?

8. What kind of a personality would you have if you were starting today? Would you be more assertive, less assertive? Would you be more nervous, less nervous? Would you be more outgoing, more inward or introverted? If you were choosing it today, what would make up your personality, the kind of person you are? Remind yourself that's exactly what you do every single day—you choose your personality.

9. How would you describe yourself, if you couldn't use any labels? I talked about this earlier in the book, but if you didn't have time to think about it then, please do so now. Without listing your age, occupation, family members, religious affiliation, financial worth, and so forth, how would you describe who you truly are?

Are you able to describe yourself without labels, or are you unable to go beyond their limitations? Can you define what it means to be you as a human being?

Those questions are a good wrap-up to what I've discussed in this book. I hope you've learned that no matter who you are, you can be someone who is so in charge that you can always trust your instincts, be childlike, be creative, do anything that makes sense to you, soar like an eagle, and live the life of your dreams.

I'd like to return to Voltaire for a moment. He was a man who took on kings and queens and really satirized everyone. Voltaire's biographer said this of him, and I feel so strongly about it I would like it to be said of me: "First and above all else, he was marvelously alive, and mankind, which dreads boredom even more than anxiety, is eternally grateful to those who make life throb to a swifter, stronger beat."

That resonates so deeply for me. If I can make your life and mine throb to a swifter, stronger beat, in what I say and what I write and what I do, there's my sense of purpose. I don't focus on external motivators anymore. I focus on what I'm doing and what I believe in, I live my mission, and all the other stuff gets taken care of. *It simply gets taken care of.*

It's all so perfect, if we only stop to realize it is. As I look at all of the self-defeating behaviors out there, I think the biggest one is found in looking outside ourselves for the secret to happiness. I have learned that there is no way to happiness. Happiness itself is the way.

JOURNAL EXERCISE

In your journal, write down your answers to the questions posed in this chapter. Then, when you have an uninterrupted chunk of time, go back over your journal and read everything you have written. From the vantage point you have now, as someone who has read and really experienced this book, how do you feel about what you've written? Do you see that you have already begun to reframe your thinking? If not, how do you think you can get in the habit of doing so?

Finally, jot down any other thoughts you have about how you might be able to work with what you already have to manifest a life of ultimate health, fulfillment, joy, passion, growth, serenity, and love—the life of your dreams.

ABOUT THE AUTHOR

Affectionately called the "father of motivation" by his fans, **Dr. Wayne W. Dyer** was an internationally renowned author, speaker, and pioneer in the field of self-development. Over the four decades of his career, he wrote more than 40 books (21 of which became *New York Times* bestsellers), created numerous audio programs and videos, and appeared on thousands of television and radio shows. His books *Manifest Your Destiny, Wisdom of the Ages, There's a Spiritual Solution to Every Problem,* and the *New York Times* bestsellers *10 Secrets for Success and Inner Peace, The Power of Intention, Living an Inspired Life, Change Your Thoughts—Change Your Life, Excuses Begone!, Wishes Fulfilled,* and *I Can See Clearly Now* were all featured as National Public Television specials.

Wayne held a doctorate in educational counseling from Wayne State University, had been an associate professor at St. John's University in New York, and honored a lifetime commitment to learning and finding the Higher Self. In 2015, he left his body, returning to Infinite Source to embark on his next adventure.

Website: www.DrWayneDyer.com

HAY HOUSE TITLES OF RELATED INTEREST

YOU CAN HEAL YOUR LIFE, the movie,
starring Louise Hay & Friends
(available as a 1-DVD program, an expanded 2-DVD set,
and an online streaming video)
Learn more at www.hayhouse.com/louise-movie

THE SHIFT, the movie,
starring Dr. Wayne W. Dyer
(available as a 1-DVD program, an expanded 2-DVD set,
and an online streaming video)
Learn more at www.hayhouse.com/the-shift-movie

*Everything Is Here to Help You: A Loving Guide to
Your Soul's Evolution,* by Matt Kahn

*The Pursuit of Dreams: Claim Your Power, Follow Your Heart,
and Fulfill Your Destiny,* by Dr. Dragos Bratasanu

*Trust Life: Love Yourself Every Day with Wisdom
from Louise Hay,* by Louise Hay

*You Be You: Detox Your Life, Transcend Your Limitations,
and Own Your Awesome,* by Drew Canole

All of the above are available at your local bookstore,
or may be ordered by contacting Hay House (see next page).

We hope you enjoyed this Hay House book. If you'd like to receive our online catalog featuring additional information on Hay House books and products, or if you'd like to find out more about the Hay Foundation, please contact:

Hay House, Inc., P.O. Box 5100, Carlsbad, CA 92018-5100
(760) 431-7695 or (800) 654-5126
(760) 431-6948 (fax) or (800) 650-5115 (fax)
www.hayhouse.com® • www.hayfoundation.org

———

Published in Australia by: Hay House Australia Pty. Ltd.,
18/36 Ralph St., Alexandria NSW 2015
Phone: 612-9669-4299 • *Fax:* 612-9669-4144
www.hayhouse.com.au

Published in the United Kingdom by: Hay House UK, Ltd.,
The Sixth Floor, Watson House, 54 Baker Street, London W1U 7BU
Phone: +44 (0)20 3927 7290 • *Fax:* +44 (0)20 3927 7291
www.hayhouse.co.uk

Published in India by: Hay House Publishers India,
Muskaan Complex, Plot No. 3, B-2, Vasant Kunj, New Delhi 110 070
Phone: 91-11-4176-1620 • *Fax:* 91-11-4176-1630
www.hayhouse.co.in

———

<u>Access New Knowledge.</u>
<u>Anytime. Anywhere.</u>

Learn and evolve at your own pace
with the world's leading experts.